Till Gay Do Us Part

One Woman's Journey
Of
Love, Betrayal, and Survival

www.advbookstore.com

Gerty Shipmaker

Till Gay Do Us Part by Gerty Shipmaker
Copyright © 2010 by Gerty Shipmaker
All Rights Reserved.
ISBN: 1-59755-249-6
ISBN13: 978-1-59755-249-3

Published by: ADVANTAGE BOOKS™
　　　　www.advbookstore.com

Scriptures taken from the Holy Bible, New International
Version®, NIV®. Copyright © 1973, 1978, 1984 by Biblica,
Inc.™ Used by permission of Zondervan. All rights reserved
worldwide. www.zondervan.com

Library of Congress Control Number: 2010937383

Cover design by Becky Shuert

First Printing: October 2010
10 11 12 13 14 15 16　10 9 8 7 6 5 4 3 2 1
Printed in the United States of America

To my children
Sarah, Deborah, Caitlin and Connor,
the ones that shared my journey,
gave me a reason to get out of bed each morning,
and made me forever thankful
for the marriage that gave me them.
I love you.
For always.

Gerty Shipmaker

Acknowledgements

There are so many people to thank. Not so much for this book finally seeing print, but for their part in the lives contained in this book.

My first thanks have to go to my children. You truly gave me the strength to go on, giving me a reason for each day. You endured pain that no child should have to endure and shouldered burdens that so often were not yours to shoulder. I have watched as you each have taken your own journey and come through on the other side gracefully. I love you more than words can say, and I am so proud to be your mom.

To my dad, thank you for all the support you and mom have been through all those years. I know that you both experienced your own pain from my journey, yet you were always there for me and the kids. While it saddens me that mom is not here to see the book that she asked about continuously, I know that she would be proud. She was my biggest fan. Thank you for being the parents you were to me.

To Jane and Case, Margaret and Wally, Rita and Bert, Jacob and Pat (my siblings and in-laws), thank you for all the small and big things you did for me. From buying Connor skates and bringing me Froot Loops and wine to helping me finance a new home, your involvement in my life was immense. For all the support, the phone calls and yes, even the tears, thank you.

To all my friends, too many to list here, both close and far away, you were a huge part of my journey. You prayed without ceasing; you cared without limits; you hugged with all your hearts. Just a phone call away, I knew you were there for me. Without your support and strength this journey would have looked a whole lot different. You know who you are.

To Ingrid, my strongest prayer warrior, my weeping partner, my confidante, my encourager. You pushed me and pulled me, sat with me, journeyed with me. Thank you, my friend.

To my Shippy, my love. Even I don't have the right words to tell you how much I love you and thank you. You have been my supporter, my shoulder, my strength, and even my editor. You have wept with me as I shared my journey and helped me come to terms with so much of it. You married me, baggage and all, accepted my children as your children and encouraged me to tell my story. I look forward to the next 40 years with you (you promised!).

Chapter 1

I was lying on the floor, stretched out in the hallway, scrunched against the wall beside the bathroom door wishing myself invisible, just waiting. Most of the lights were out, creating a creepy kind of semi-darkness which was perfect for what I was about to do.

I could hear John, my husband of just over a year, finishing up in the bathroom and I lay as quiet as possible. No giggling, not even in anticipation of winning this round. This was serious work, and I wasn't about to mess up with any sounds. If I could have, I would have held my breath, but I knew if I did that I was liable to pass out. Then he'd come out of the bathroom and step on my head which would defeat the purpose of what I was doing there in the first place.

And so I breathed.

Exactly as expected John opened the bathroom door. As he did, he automatically turned off the light, putting us in complete darkness. Perfect. Just as he stepped out into the hallway I reached out and grabbed his ankle quickly and firmly.

It couldn't have been any better, I thought, as this grown man began to scream and yell and jump up and down trying to get away from the grip of his terror. My grip. Of course in all his hysterical commotion he didn't even realize his ankle had been let go and his wife was rolling around laughing maniacally.

I had won.

I had successfully scared him almost to death.

Of course I knew there would be revenge, but I was sure this moment would be worth it.

I was a little less sure when we had both calmed down and were lying side by side in bed. Not touching but not sleeping. Chuckling again, I began to speak to him, but he didn't answer.

"John?"

No response.

Oh-oh. No, he wouldn't get back at me so soon. That's not the way we played the game. So I tried again.

"John? Answer me, please."

The logical thing to do at this point, of course, was to reach out and touch him, but by then I had successfully scared myself to the point of being frozen to the bed. There was not a logical thought in my head. I literally couldn't move.

"I'm sorry, John, okay? I'll never do it again. Can we stop playing this game now?"

No response.

Only a few seconds passed in total and complete fear. Suddenly there was a slight movement beside me and a voice right beside my ear whispered, "Boo."

I burst into tears and proceeded to sob and shake uncontrollably.

It was John's turn to laugh the victory laugh. I became inconsolable. How could he be so mean, so horrid, so scary?

Yet that was what it was all about. I have no idea how this strange and twisted game began but there was only one goal and no rules. The goal was simply to scare the other person. It was so difficult for me to actually scare him because often in the process I'd spook myself and quit.

John, however, was very good at this game. Many times we would lie in bed having a conversation when he would suddenly get quiet. I knew instinctively that another round of "the game" had begun. I knew that I was about to get spooked and simply knowing that I was going to get spooked, spooked me.

There were times that he wasn't actually planning anything; he would be simply be thinking, but by the time he would reach out to hug me his touch would cause me to come unglued. I always cried.

On some level I hated it, this game, but on another level it was one of those quirky things that bonded us closer together. A stupid little game, but it was ours alone, and it made us laugh (after my tears of course).

We continued to play it over the early years of our marriage. Until one day we knew it had gone too far.

This particular scaring incident also happened outside a bathroom door, but in a new home. This bathroom door was to our ensuite. It was a simple bifold door, solid on the bottom with angled slats on the top. John was inside brushing his teeth and I was standing about half an inch on the outside able to peek in through those slats and know when he would be coming out, knowing he couldn't see me, nor expect me to be standing there.

It was perfect.

Taking the idea straight from a page of his own game manual, when he opened the door I simply said, "Boo." I didn't say it loud or dramatically; I didn't move as I said it; I didn't laugh. I don't even think it was dark. Just a simple "Boo."

But what registered was not a little "Boo" from his beautiful wife. Instead something in his mind told him he was being attacked, and testosterone began to run wild in him. Without thinking that most attackers don't announce themselves with a quiet "Boo," and without even noticing who it was that was standing there ready to attack him, he brought up his arm while clenching his fist. His shoulder went back, and his whole body began to move in towards the punch that he was aiming at his enemy of the moment.

Which was me!

It all happened so fast that it didn't really occur to me in those split seconds that he was feeling threatened by me. All I saw was my husband ready to punch me.

At the last possible moment something registered in his mind, and he realized who I was. Fortunately he then chose to drop his arm. We both just stood there staring at each other and knew "the game" was over.

Forever.

Not in my wildest dreams would I have thought that roughly 20 years later I would discover that he had been playing a completely different game with me. A game where only I was in the dark. One with no winners, no victory dance, only terror and tears.

Chapter 2

I was at a crossroads in my life. Having finished one year of college and recently ending a one-year-long engagement, I was working in a bakery while I tried to figure out my future.

Working the Friday evening shift, it was a quiet night at the bakery when a tall, dark, and handsome man walked in. I immediately recognized him from church and so I smiled (I like to think prettily) as I said, "Hi, Bob."

There was an awkward silence while he looked at me strangely. If I had to guess I would say he was weighing his options. Finally he spoke. "Uh, Bob's my brother. My name is John."

So much for the immediate recognition, but at least I had the right family.

Moving past my embarrassment, we chatted for a few minutes and it became apparent that he wasn't interested in buying anything. But because there was no one else waiting (and the boss was gone) I continued visiting with him.

Just when I was about to wonder what he was actually doing there, he asked me if I would go out on a date with him. Woo-hoo!! Even though I had only been officially single again for five weeks, I was 19 years old, and in our circles that was marrying age, so there was no time to lose.

He mentioned a day the following week and without any thought I agreed. It wasn't until after he had gone that I started to think about it, and I realized that I already had plans for that same night, plans that I couldn't change. I had committed myself to helping my dad with an organ concert on that evening.

Let me explain. My dad is a musician, but more specifically he is a church organist, playing since he was 16 years old on big pipe organs in Holland. After immigrating to Canada, he became the church organist and choir director of the church in Chilliwack, where my parents had decided to live. In the days when pipe organs reigned (yes, extending well past my teen years), he often brought guest organists from Holland to put on concerts. I enjoyed not only the concerts, but having the organists stay at our home, helping out with parties after the concerts, and giving a hand with whatever was needed during the concert.

There wasn't even a thought in my head that I would miss the concert or not help my parents just so I could go on a date. I called John and told him that I had a conflicting schedule for our first date and told him what I was committed to. He must have really wanted to go out with me because he suggested we go out a little later, after the concert. Not wanting to miss an opportunity for a first date, knowing that without the first there wouldn't likely be a second, I heartily agreed.

The evening came and I collected tickets with my mom and enjoyed the concert with both my parents, probably a little more exuberantly than usual, knowing that I was going out with John later on. I was helping serve coffee back at home for all the friends my parents had invited back to the house when John arrived.

It was 9:30 p.m. by the time we left. It would have been prudent for me at that time to let John in on some details regarding my family. He already knew that I was the youngest of four girls and that all my older sisters were successfully married (in our world married meant successful).

What I hadn't told him was that my sisters had already run the route of dating before me, and the rules were firmly entrenched by the time I entered that phase. And by entrenched rules, I mean unbreakable, not even bendable, set in stone kind of rules. My parents made them and my sisters and I knew them; it was even common knowledge amongst many of our peers.

I should have made sure John knew them.

You see, curfew was 11 p.m. Period. There were no exceptions (that I can recall) and there was never a good reason to be late. Even worse than being late (if you dared) was getting lost in time while sitting in the driveway in the car because then, at the stroke of 11 p.m., the front porch light would begin flashing. There was nothing more embarrassing than sitting in the car with a date when the porch light screamed, "It's 11 o'clock, and you had better get yourself in the house!" More so because we girls knew that our dad was on the other side of the door with his hand on the switch.

In his underwear.

I'm not sure if it was fear of breaking curfew or fear of dad coming through that door in his underwear and ruining our lives forever, but whenever the porch light flashed, each of his daughters was in the house within minutes.

None of this information, however, seemed quite first date material to chat about, so I chose not to mention any of it to John when he picked me up.

For our first date, he took me to a little pub where we got to know each other better. Thoroughly enjoying myself, curfew flew out of my head. Now many things would be welcome to fly out of my head, but curfew? A very, very bad thing to fly out.

It wasn't until we left the pub that curfew flew back in and I realized it was likely a good thing we were on our way out because it must be getting close to my witching hour. I was thinking that with any luck I'd be home on time, sparing myself what I thought would be an embarrassing confession – telling my date that I had to be home by 11 p.m.

Crossing the parking lot, I lit up a cigarette. Smoking was a nasty habit that I had picked up in elementary school and by this time I was a pack-a-day smoker. Happily, and perhaps obliviously, I walked to the passenger side of John's car and waited for him to come and unlock the door.

"Gerty," I heard John say. "You can't smoke in my car. Sorry."

I looked at him. "Seriously?" I asked.

"Seriously."

Wow. For just a minute I wondered what kind of strange creature John was. There was no one I knew that didn't allow smoking in their vehicle; it had been years since my parents had told me I wasn't allowed to smoke, and up until then I think they were the only ones that had ever prohibited it (well, they and those elementary school teachers).

I was taken aback and quite embarrassed. In any other scenario I would have likely thought he was a jerk and left him standing there. Two things prevented that. One, I really liked this guy, and two, it was a long walk home, dark, and I was more than a little paranoid of going anywhere alone in the dark.

I looked at my freshly lit cigarette and at the object of my freshly begun relationship and wisely put out my cigarette.

Figuring I'd still make it home reasonably close to curfew, I wasn't sure at first how to answer John when he suggested we go for a hot chocolate. What I should have done at that point was tell him that I really needed to get home. Instead I opened my mouth and said I'd love to go for a hot chocolate.

I was having such a good time, enjoying John's sense of humour and the way we were able to talk so comfortably that I figured whatever consequences there were to breaking curfew would be worth it.

We ended up at McDonald's, which suddenly became a very romantic place to me.

John was appearing to be almost perfect. Well, except for the not smoking in his car incident, that is. He seemed like my knight in shining armour. Granted, he had a perm and was wearing a turtleneck, but compared to the flannel and denim of the farming crowd I normally hung out with, that was just a nice change.

So there we were. Nearing the end of our first date, I had already called him by the wrong name, tried to smoke in his car, and even though he didn't know it yet, I had withheld information that might get him expelled from the good graces of my dad (which he had yet to earn).

I didn't exactly give him the best impression of myself.

We picked up our hot chocolate and found a booth. I took the lid off my hot chocolate and began to stir it. John, on the other hand, didn't seem to see a need for a stir stick and began to shake his.

You might think that that should work, seeing as it had a lid on it. Unfortunately, it did not. Because, in the next few seconds, the lid flew off his drink and hot chocolate exploded all over the table, the window, and the wall.

As I watched the rivers of chocolate drip down all around me, I suddenly wasn't quite so worried about any bad impressions that I had made.

It was well after midnight when he brought me home. As we pulled up to the front of the house I noticed that people were still visiting. I wasn't sure if this boded well for my sneaking in, or if I would be the center of everyone's attention as I got busted for breaking curfew. The only thing I was very sure of was that dad wouldn't be standing on the other side of the door in his underwear (yes, I was counting my blessings).

I nervously entered the house and was greeted warmly by my parents and their friends. In a rare historical family moment, I had succeeded in getting away with breaking curfew.

After all the guests left, I stood at the kitchen counter helping mom clean up. I told her that I was going to marry John.

Good thing he asked me out again.

We began to date, spending much of our spare time together. We went for long walks through the city, down the railway tracks and through parks, having great conversations. We told each other about our lives, our passions, our dreams; we had lively discussions about God, church, and our beliefs. We never seemed to run out of things to say.

Very early in our relationship he took me to Stanley Park in Vancouver where we walked the park and the seven kilometre (km) seawall. As we were walking along, he suddenly bent over, picked a flower, and gave it to me. It was bright yellow and very pretty. I was all gushy and happy inside, thinking he must be the most romantic man I had ever met. I smiled at him.

He smile back and said, oh so sweetly, "That's skunk cabbage, you know."

I didn't know, but I did know that 'skunk' and 'cabbage' were not pretty words so I quickly threw it out. He would tease me about that for years.

As we were driving out of the park that afternoon, he gave me the first of what would be many thoughtful gifts during our relationship. This one was a stuffed animal; more specifically a bright blue Grover, one of the muppets from a children's television show. I had told him how I loved Grover (I had a much younger brother, in case you are wondering why I was attached to a children's television show character). He was just so adorable when he would say in his broken voice, "Hello, it is I, furry loveable old Grover."

We (John and I, not Grover and I) quickly became best friends and almost inseparable. In addition to our long walks where we talked about anything and everything, he regularly sent me flowers, usually yellow roses. (Memories of the skunk cabbage perhaps?) He would often cook meals for me in his apartment and he took me to see my first movie in a theatre, *Grease*.

It was a different world back then. Those were the days of one movie in town for a week, so it wasn't something people went to on a nightly basis. For some reason our family just didn't do much movie going. My parents went to the occasional one with their friends, but it simply wasn't a regular thing in our lives.

I remember that first movie, not only because it was a musical and based in the fifties (the decade that I am more fascinated by than any other), but because my dad had given me an ultimatum earlier in the evening. I had not been making it home by curfew every night and my parents were not impressed. That evening I was told to tell John that I had a curfew or my dad would.

I really don't need to say that the choice here was obvious; there was no way on earth that I could allow my dad to tell John to bring me home by 11 p.m. and so I squirmed through much of that movie, angry that my dad was enforcing such a dumb rule and worried about how I would look when I told John.

I finally just blurted it out. "I have an eleven o'clock curfew."

Thinking we would be entering into some sort of dialogue about the stupidity of a curfew, or how I should have told him sooner, I was surprised when he replied, "Oh, I know that. I was just waiting for you to tell me."

Now there were two men I was angry with.

Two months later, after another evening out together, John walked me to the door as he usually did. Stopping just shy of the front door, John leaned back against the pillar on the front porch and pulled me toward him. We were saying good-bye; my arms were around his neck and his around my waist.

John looked down at my face and into my eyes. "Will you marry me?" he quietly asked.

With no hesitation on my part whatsoever, I answered simply, "Yes."

And so we began a new stage, planning the happy-ever-after part of our lives.

Chapter 3

Something John and I shared right from the beginning of our relationship was our commitment to our church. We had both grown up within the same denomination and enjoyed going to church.

I loved our church. I loved the familiarity of hearing the Ten Commandments each week, listening to good preachers, hearing my dad play the big pipe organ, and the majestic sound of hundreds of people singing with all their hearts (to this day, I have not heard congregational singing like what I grew up hearing). I even enjoyed being part of the choir (even when we had to wear those huge burgundy robes that made us look fat).

One of the things John had told me about himself in one of our first dates was that he couldn't sing, that he was tone deaf. I had never met anyone that couldn't sing, so I didn't believe him. I presumed that he was simply a shy singer, maybe not always hitting the correct note.

It was the first time that we went to church as a couple. We stood up ready to sing the first hymn, opened the hymnbook, and waited for the end of the organ's introduction. When we heard our cue, we burst into the opening notes.

Or at least I did. But that was about all I could get out. I couldn't help but hear the most horrific notes (or lack thereof) coming from John's lips. I simply stopped singing and stared at him, like he was from another planet.

He stopped as well, but only to look back at me. Maybe my mouth was open, I don't know. Not needing an explanation for why I was staring at him, he simply said, "I told you I was tone deaf." I have to say I was a little embarrassed for him, but I was also pleased to know that he would still sing no matter how he sounded.

As much as I enjoyed going to church, when I was on my own in the quiet times in bed at night, I felt like I was missing something. The whole going to church thing didn't quite seem to fill that part of me that I thought it should. I would pull out my bible at night and look at it. I thought I should probably read it, but I didn't really know how to begin, or where to begin, or what I should be looking for. Did I doubt God? No, I believed in His existence completely. I knew the Bible was His word, the truth; I just didn't seem to know what to do with it.

So I just stared at it a lot and pondered it all.

That yearning had been with me for several years. I just knew there had to be more to believing in God that I wasn't getting. I continued to look almost longingly at my bible. I might have opened it on occasion, but it would have been a rare one. It never occurred to me to ask anyone what I was missing; I was pretty sure it was something I should have already understood by then.

Months went by, and we were getting close to our spring wedding. One night I was lying in my bed, again contemplating it all, when I truly felt God calling me. It wasn't an audible calling, but a strong sensation that I needed to respond to Him; that I had to make a choice of sorts.

The feeling was so strong that I just couldn't ignore it, but wasn't entirely sure how to respond to it either, so I responded with two words. "Yes, Jesus," was all I said.

"Yes, Jesus." Those two words were what I consider the beginning of my walk with the Lord. Not a conventional walk, but not doing things in the normal way was, for me, quite normal.

I said those words, "Yes, Jesus," and felt a peace, a knowledge that I had responded correctly. Just six weeks before we were married, I publicly confessed my faith in Him in front of our church. I had no idea what that would mean or where it would lead me. God would, in fact, carry the entire relationship on those two small words for the next four years.

Chapter 4

As the weeks flew by, bringing us closer and closer to our wedding, I grew more and more in love with John. In a journal entry, written just months before our wedding, I wrote: *John is, and always will be, everything I want in a husband. He's kind, sincere, beautiful, thoughtful, and everything else nice. He's not afraid to say what he feels or that he feels.*

There was only one thing that was a cause for a problem between us: my smoking. John hated it that I smoked, and I repeatedly tried to quit over the months that we dated. It was just weeks before our wedding that I put out my last cigarette and never smoked again, ending a 10-year addiction.

Then came the spring evening when my dad walked me down the aisle on our wedding day. I was wearing a long white gown that my mom had made, its 14-foot train carried by my nephew and niece. My sisters, all dressed in floor-length pink dresses, also created by mom, were my bridesmaids. At the end of that aisle stood the love of my life, as handsome as ever in his tuxedo, waiting for me.

As per the tradition of our community of that time, we had a Friday evening candlelight wedding. It was followed by a reception with light food, all of which my parents made. We sang songs, people performed skits, and we cut the cake (made by my dad, who spent many years of his life as a baker).

Fourteen months after our first date, we were finally married. I felt complete, having married my best friend.

After a short honeymoon spent by the ocean on the Oregon coast, we moved to Rossland, a community 500 km away from our family. Nestled in the mountains in the West Kootenays of British Columbia, Rossland was a one-stoplight town, and that light was only a flashing one. John had accepted a job with the Credit Union as an accountant while doing correspondence courses towards getting his Certified General Accountant (CGA) degree.

We found ourselves an apartment just minutes away from Red Mountain, a well-known, beautiful ski hill. We didn't have much in that first home, and, in fact, slept on a mattress on the floor with milk crates for bedside tables.

I loved those early days of our marriage. Following our own parents' example, we got up together every morning. I wouldn't go so far as to say that I cooked breakfast or anything, since getting up, in and of itself, was quite enough for me to do at that time of day. (If you've ever seen the cartoon that says, "I may rise, but I refuse to shine" then you've seen me.) I hate mornings. God and I would have many words about why he had to make them (and years later, he would have the last laugh). Nonetheless, each morning John and I would sit down and eat toast and drink tea before he'd go off to work.

Every day he'd come home for lunch.

Most evenings, after dinner, we'd go for a walk. Hand in hand, we explored our new city for hours while we talked about the future: John's career plans, the children we'd like to have some day, a trip to Europe that we dreamed of taking, the houses we liked, and the plans that John had to build our own house. We shared our thoughts about our faith and concerns about finding a church and making new friends.

While it was lonely at times, being away from all of our family and everything we knew, we settled into our life as a married couple. After several weeks I found a job in the bakery department of a grocery store in Trail, a city 10 km away, and there I met Arlo, my first friend since moving.

Arlo was one of the bakers and a few years older than me. He was not much taller than me, not much heavier, and seemed to walk around with a grin on his face, always looking to crack a joke or pull a prank on someone. (In some ways he reminded me of my dad in his younger years, dressed in the traditional white pants, shirt, and hat of bakers and sharing the same sense of humour.) We hit it off as friends almost immediately and very quickly I discovered that he, too, lived in Rossland and that he and his wife, Linda, lived in our apartment building just two floors below us.

Arlo and Linda were married one year longer than us, had not yet begun a family, and all four of us worked (Linda was an elementary school teacher), so it wasn't long before the four of us began hanging out in the evenings and sometimes on the weekends. Arlo loved adventure and would take us all four-wheeling in the back country in their jeep, terrifying me as he tried to go over logs and through places not meant for vehicles. In the winter he'd ski in places not meant for skiers, loving activities that had an element of danger.

Working with Arlo most days and spending much of our free time together as couples, it didn't take long before they convinced us to come to church with them. Up until that point we had been drifting around trying to find a church similar to the one we'd left back home. We were finding it very difficult to find one where we felt like we could fit in. One Sunday in particular we drove for over an hour to attend what we thought would be a traditional church that would be comfortable for us. I suppose the town was quite a touristy one, or perhaps it had an "outreach to the beach" program, I don't know, but there were more people in church dressed in shorts and t-shirts than in dresses and suits like we were. Some even carried towels under their arms, ready to hit the beach at the final "Amen." One t-shirt in particular made us realize this church was a little too casual for us. Blazoned across this person's chest was "Party till you puke."

We both felt strongly that we needed to find a place to worship where we lived, and so when Arlo and Linda invited us to go along with them to the Alliance church in Trail, we decided to give it a try. A little nervously, we went with them that first Sunday, the only Sunday where the congregation was without a pastor. One had just preached his last sermon the week previously, and the new pastor wouldn't be arriving until the following week. As such, they had a singing group come in and it was an hour of straight worship. Although we were a little shocked when the Ten Commandments weren't read, only one offering was taken, and nobody handed out peppermints during the service, we still enjoyed ourselves.

At least everyone was dressed the same way we were.

There were many young couples and young families with us in the pews and everyone was very welcoming, so we made the decision to keep attending there for the time being.

There were many adjustments for us going to an unfamiliar church; a less structured, less traditional denomination. We spent many hours discussing theology and doctrine with Arlo and Linda and then with others whom we got to know at church.

I struggled with issues of faith. I didn't understand why anything more than attending church and praying before and after eating was required (something that was done faithfully in my home growing up). I didn't see that a 'sinner's prayer' and a special request was needed for me to be a Christian. What was with these people that they took it all so personally, I wondered, having it invade every part of their lives? Did that mean I wasn't as good a Christian? I had been baptized as a baby, I publicly professed my faith and became a member of my church back home. Wasn't that was enough?

And so the discussions continued.

John and I spent more and more time discussing God, our faith, and our future, usually while walking in the evenings. It was in those quiet times together that we began to rethink our plans for the future. We had always thought that we would only stay in Rossland for two years. Most of that decision was wrapped up in our church and wanting (perhaps even needing) to be rooted back in the denomination of our upbringing before we had children. Now we were wondering at the importance of a particular denomination, if the type of church mattered as much as we thought. These were huge issues for us.

As we wavered on the edge of staying or moving on before we had children, we bought a mobile home. The emphasis for us then was the mobile part, thinking that we could stay or leave while owning our own home.

While John was studying to be an accountant and working as one at the credit union, in reality he was a frustrated architect. He loved reading home plan and architectural magazines and designing houses in his spare time. He had an eye for design and so it wasn't a surprise that, shortly after we moved into our mobile home, he wanted to improve it.

As did most mobile homes in that era, ours had dark wall paneling. Neither of us liked it much, and so we decided to wallpaper over it in the living room.

Wallpapering brought back happy memories for me. Growing up, every wall in our house was wallpapered. Several times, in fact. I realize that as we grow older our memory is not always accurate, but I'm pretty sure that on those nights that I managed to get in the house after a date and before the underwear and flashing lights happened, I would always find my dad wallpapering. And I think it was almost always the hallway that he was re-wallpapering. There was the black plastic trough on the floor, a ladder beside it, a pair of scissors, and my dad holding a wet strip of paper. I remember red velvet printed paper, gold, green, and cream paper, and stripes, prints, and patterns. That hallway was re-papered so often, I'm pretty sure it was a few feet narrower by the time I moved out of the house.

All that to say that I was all over the idea of wallpapering with John, seeing as I was the one with all that experience in my family. I figured I must know all there was to know.

It was a simple concept, a simple job.

John, on the other hand, had not wallpapered before. Not even osmosisly (yes, I know that is not a word...or wasn't before now). For some reason he did not want to bow to my expertise and thought it would be prudent to read the instructions.

I insisted I knew what I was doing.

He insisted on reading the instructions.

Words were exchanged, and it got a little intense, which is, of course, a polite way of saying we had a fight.

John proceeded to read the instructions, and I proceeded to refuse to speak to him.

He began papering. I began sulking. He appeared to be doing a decent job for a novice, but still I wouldn't help. It was while he was cutting off the bottom edge of one strip of paper that a hammer that had, just seconds before, been resting on the top of a chair now fell down and hit him on the head. In hindsight, I do have to wonder why there was a hammer there at all, not remembering that being part of my childhood wallpapering experience. Nonetheless, it had been there on the chair, and then it was there on the floor after bouncing off of John's head.

Oh, the words that came out of the mouth of my husband! Among them was an accusation that I had tried to kill him. Even though I was nowhere near that hammer before, during, or after it fell, he seriously thought I had tried to kill him.

As I looked at him and listened to his accusations, I think he was lucky that there wasn't a hammer close to me at that particular moment.

There is always a lesson to be learned through experiences such as this, and we learned one that day that stayed with us throughout our marriage, that being to never wallpaper together, and even though many of the walls in the homes we lived in over the years to follow were wallpapered, it was never hung together.

As we settled into our home and into our church, we began to think more and more about setting down roots in Rossland. We had made many good friends, were involved in the community, and very much enjoyed our life there.

We continued to dream about going to Europe, more specifically Holland, where most of my extended family still lived, and we wanted to do that before we had a family.

With our second anniversary not far away, we decided to make the trip. My parents agreed to come with us for the first part of the trip and then we'd be on our own for the last bit. I was so excited, I sewed myself a new skirt, blouse, and jacket for the occasion (some people buy luggage, I sewed myself an outfit...I should have bought luggage). I will remember that outfit forever because I wasn't much of a seamstress at that time, and I made the jacket and the blouse to fit perfectly. Perfectly, that is, until I had to move my arms. I had not given myself any room to move, and as such it wasn't in the least bit comfortable. I wore it anyway.

A few weeks before we left on our month-long trip one of us suggested that, just for fun, and just for one night, we try to conceive a baby, throwing caution (and birth control) to the wind. Our plans were to start our family when we got back from Europe, so this simply seemed like a spontaneous and fun idea.

I don't know which one of us had the original idea, but the other agreed (okay, I'm pretty sure that it was my suggestion, and I'm pretty sure the only thing John heard was, "blah, blah, blah, sex tonight, blah, blah, blah" and, of course, agreed). We ran down the hall to our bedroom laughing together at the spontaneity of what we were doing.

After that night, we didn't think too much more about it in the excitement of our trip.

It was at my grandparents' home in Holland that I suspected we'd succeeded at conceiving a child, but also knew that my body could just be reacting to travel stress. When I slept the entire way through England, I seriously suspected my stress might eventually end up with a name. So it was that on the boat from Dover, England to wherever we were going that we shared the news with my parents.

"You are what?!"

"Did you plan this?"

"Why didn't you wait?"

"Well, that's exciting, I guess."

Not exactly the reaction we were hoping for, but we were too excited to really be bothered by it. Just in case I wasn't sure, it was confirmed when we returned to my grandparents home. My Opa was smoking his usual pipe, at his usual time of 7 a.m., creating a pretty blue haze in the living room. Normally I loved the smell of his pipe and it made me want to hug my Opa each morning. Now, however, I only wanted to vomit.

I was most definitely pregnant. My grandmother, a pregnancy professional, having birthed 17 of her own children, said she knew it from the beginning.

After four beautiful weeks in Europe we came home tired but excited. The trip had been everything we hoped for, and now we were beginning another journey.

We were having a baby.

Chapter 5

Not too many years after that spontaneous conception we were driving through Spokane, Washington on a family vacation. We were now driving a station wagon; that alone tells you how carried away things got once we started this family thing.

Between John and I in the front seat sat one small child, behind us sat three more children, the oldest eight, the youngest almost three.

Four children.

Four.

Back in the days when John and I took those wonderful walks together, we talked about having four children. Both of us grew up as one of five children. Having a large family seemed like a great idea.

But four children in six years? How did that happen? Well, okay, I know how it happened. After all, I was there.

But seriously, how?

Okay, so we planned the first, if you call a suggestion and a dash down the hall planning, and as a result we had a beautiful daughter we named Sarah.

We planned our second one as well, although that was more of a "yeah, like, whatever" moment. Deborah, another beautiful daughter, was born 21 months after Sarah.

After that we began to rethink our plans. We were no longer so sure we wanted four children, but if we were to have more than the two we thought it best to wait several years then maybe have two more. We were still living in our mobile home and two children seemed almost over the limit for our small two-bedroom dwelling. I had my hands full that winter.

Ah, winter in Rossland. Winter often began in October, sometimes having snow as early as October 3, and often staying until the end of April. The average annual snowfall in Rossland is 370 cm, or 12 feet. While I absolutely love winter, and the more snow the better, when Deborah was born in the middle of October it did make for a challenge with two little ones. Because we used a wood stove for heat, the living room was the warmest place to bathe the baby to keep her little toes from getting frostbite (ice coated the edges of the windows and French doors at the front and the back of our mobile). Life got a bit "squashed" in the winter months in our home. Walks with the girls were almost not possible on my own, and I often would feel quite housebound.

I simply couldn't imagine where we would put a third child, or how I could manage with another.

Therefore we weren't planning a third child.

When Sarah was two and a half years old and Deborah not yet having celebrated her first birthday, I missed a period. I was still breastfeeding, so I didn't give much thought to it, but then my parents decided to come for a visit. We would often have a glass of wine together when they came over, so I decided to make sure I wasn't pregnant before they came. There were no home pregnancy tests in those days, so I went to my doctor for a pregnancy test. While it was long past the days of testing for pregnancy with a rabbit, I did still have to go into the clinic and give a urine sample.

My doctor took that sample and placed some in a special little vial. Together he and I sat watching the little vial as he turned it around and around. I know, rather a disgusting thought now, watching your own pee swirl in a vial, but that was just the way it was tested to find out if you were pregnant. As I watched intently, I had no idea what I was looking for, but I watched nonetheless as if my life were depending on it, expecting it to tell me that I was not pregnant.

I swear we watched that vial for hours, if not days.

Finally the doctor looked up from the vial. I kept looking at it. I don't know why, I think it was just safer. "Well!" he exclaimed. I took my eyes off the vial and sat back in my seat feeling relieved. "Well" must mean that I could go home and safely enjoy a glass of wine when my parents arrived. He was probably wondering how to break the news to me that I wasn't pregnant. But then he finished his sentence. "Go home and open the champagne," he announced. "You're pregnant!"

I looked back at the vial and then looked at him.

I wanted to hurt him.

Instead, I stumbled out of the office, walked up the street, around the corner, and up the hill to the Credit Union. I promptly walked through the doors, up the stairs, and into John's office. There I just looked at him and burst into tears. Hysterical, sobbing, noisy tears. "I'm pregnant!" I cried out between the hiccups and sobs.

Every bit as shocked as I was, he took the rest of the day off so we could process the news.

I am one of those rare women who had beautiful pregnancies. I was seldom sick during my first two pregnancies, and I thoroughly enjoyed the experience. This third one was completely different. For eight months I threw up. I had hypoglycemia. For the eight months after finding out I was pregnant I dreaded what my life would look like with three children under three years old. (The only reason I didn't dread it for nine months was because I didn't know I was pregnant for the first month.)

Our third daughter was born in the middle of a raging spring storm, one that caused a house to slide right off a mountain less than a kilometre away from where she was born. We affectionately named our newest baby Condom Kid. In public, we called her Caitlin. Born at the end of May, the days were longer, the sun was warmer, and this newborn baby was the sweetest and easiest baby to have around.

Then there was our fourth child. He was kind of planned, but not completely. He began as a thought in my mind, but not in John's.

At all. For some reason I thought a fourth child would be nice (how quickly I forgot the emotions of the previous pregnancy). Caitlin was almost three years old and diapers were still a memory, but that memory was more connected with beautiful fat newborns, so I was beginning to think another baby would be nice. I was, fortunately, smart enough to know that John and I had to be in agreement in order to bring another child into the world. Nagging might have worked to get jewellery (as witnessed by the tiny diamond ring I always wore on my pinky), but it didn't seem right to nag for a baby.

Instead I prayed. It's different when you nag God; I like to think he rather expects it. I might have told God what he should do (insert lightening bolts). I told him that if he wanted us to have another baby, it would be up to him to tell John about it. I was going to back off. This backing off, in and of itself, would be a milestone for me.

Maybe God knew I'd only be able to back off and not nag for a short period of time because it wasn't long after that prayer that John came home from work and told me that it might not be a bad idea to have another baby.

In hindsight, and with great counting, we realized that our child had already been conceived when he voiced that thought. We always thought of that as a little God-moment in our lives.

Our fourth child was a son. After three girls we were given a son. Only problem with that was that I did not want a son. John was ecstatic when he was born, jumping up and down beside me, yelling, "It's a boy! It's a boy!! It's a boy!!" I wanted them to put him back. I expected a girl; I was counting on a girl. I liked girls; I understood girls.

Connor was born in the late afternoon on the last day of November. Shortly after his birth, it began to snow. That entire first night of his life it snowed. I held my beautiful newborn son and stared out the window in my hospital room most of the night. It was so peaceful and beautiful out there; all was quiet.

I stood there watching the snow fall as my own tears slid down my cheeks. I didn't know what to do with a boy, and I was terrified. I grew up with four girls, and boys were a complete unknown to me. I envisioned this little baby's teen years as hellish ones, full of drugs, drinking, and, oh horror, driving! By the morning after his arrival, I was convinced this child would be impossible to raise.

In a happy turn of events, I was quite wrong. Instead, everything stereotypical that I believed about boys was erased one small step at a time, and our family was a busy but happy one.

So there we were. The six of us in a station wagon in downtown Spokane. Each one of us was uncomfortably surrounded by, or sitting on, either camping gear or groceries. Only two hours from home, we had stopped at Costco to load up on groceries.

We were returning from three weeks of camping. Every summer we loaded up the car with gear: tarps, bedding, camp stove, lantern, buckets, a stroller, and food for our small army. Then we would head off on a trip with the kids. Some years we'd stay close to home, others we would travel as far away as Disneyland.

We all loved to go camping; we loved the tenting, exploring, hiking, and campfires. We'd make crafts out of nature, the kids would build forts in the bushes, we'd sit around the fire and roast marshmallows. The only thing missing in years previous to that particular one, in my opinion, was a guitar playing while we sat around the campfire. I mean, doesn't the ultimate campfire include a guitar and camp songs?

Well, this year it was different. I had picked up a guitar at a garage sale and had begun to teach myself to play.

By the time we went on this camping trip I had mastered three chords (G, C and D), but figured that was enough…they and my guitar came with us. I had visions of sing-a-longs around the campfire (the year was not that far from "It Only Takes a Spark" being a current song, what can I say?), and serenading my four children to sleep. The pictures in my mind were so warm and fuzzy…think Norman Rockwell slash Von Trapp singers…sigh…how could it not be perfect?

And so every night, after the kids were tucked into bed, I would sit on one of the beds and begin my serenade. It was pretty much the same each night:

"Al-le…" pause to find the G chord…"lu-ia"

"Al-le"…pause to find the C chord…"lu-ia"

"Al-le" …pause to find the D chord…"lu-ia"

"Al-le"…pause to find the G chord… "lu-ia"

That, of course, was repeated and after that followed the verses...He's my saviour….He is worthy…I will praise him. And then one more rousing repetition of the first verse, Alleluia.

My kids were either young enough to appreciate it or old enough not to tell me how painful it was, but I thoroughly enjoyed myself. I felt like I had arrived in the motherhood department. It couldn't get much more idealic than that, I thought. Funny, I don't remember John being in there with us any of those times...hmmm...

So it was at the end of those three weeks, a minimum of twenty-one glorious Alleluias later, that we were on our way home, on the last stretch, after filling every possible inch of our station wagon with the groceries we'd just bought. The sacred guitar was resting on the top behind our precious children. To say the kids were comfortable would be, well, lying.

We were looking forward to getting home, having only a couple hours of driving left when suddenly someone cut directly in front of us. John had no choice but to hit the brakes.

Hard.

Our car came to a dead stop.

The guitar, however, didn't. In fact, it just carried right on into the backs of our children's heads. Along with, and followed by, miscellaneous groceries.

In the moment that the guitar came to rest, I found out what John actually thought of that guitar and my singing...

...not much, as it turned out.

It was the first and last camping trip we had with that guitar. The kids never even asked why...

Chapter 6

By the time we had all four of our children we were firmly planted. We had made the decision to stay where we were, and just before I discovered I was pregnant with Caitlin we sold our mobile home and bought a house.

Years earlier we had bought a lot on the other side of town and John had drawn up plans to build a house for us there, but when the unique post and beam house next to our lot went up for sale we decided to check it out before we made our final decision to build. We fell in love with the house as soon as we walked in. It had beautiful wood floors, big beams, a loft, a sunken living room with a wood stove, huge windows with great views, an open floor plan, and a potential of four bedrooms. Even though we did not know that we would be having a third child soon, let alone plans for a fourth at that time, we knew this house would easily become a home that would work well for our family, and so we bought it.

We were also firmly entrenched in our church at this point, having now been there for close to ten years. The church family had become a very important part of our lives, in some ways filling the gap that was left when we moved away from our own families. This church had become the spiritual center of our lives.

For me, that part of my journey really began when Sarah was only four months old. We heard that the Sutera Twins were coming to Trail for a revival. At that point in my life, I had not carried on my original "Yes, Jesus" from before we were married to anything much deeper. Oh, I thoroughly enjoyed our church services, I loved to worship, and I dearly loved the people in our church. I definitely believed in God. But I never read the Bible on my own or had quiet times with God. That was all foreign to me.

And if quiet times with God were foreign to me, you can only imagine what a revival might have been to me. In my mind a revival was synonymous with chaos. No, I'd never been to one, but that didn't prevent me from having preconceived notions about them. The closest I might have been to what I pictured a revival to be was a service I attended at a radical Pentecostal church 10 years previously. Coming from a conservative and traditional church, where clapping to the music and raising hands were just not done, I was already quite uncomfortable when people in that Pentecostal congregation began doing exactly that during worship. When people began dancing in the aisles I was so totally out of my comfort zone that I weaved my way down the aisle and out of the church in a spiritual panic.

So when I heard that there was a revival coming to town, I imagined a good number of black people, high emotion, and people being slain in the spirit, being thumped and healed all over the place. I imagined there to be loud singing and clapping and "Praise the Lord and thank you, Jesus!!" shouted everywhere. I mean no offense to anyone, but in my ignorance that was my mental picture. In reality, I am not even sure I knew what the word revival meant, but I did know it scared me more than just a little (I liked my God in a nice orderly package).

With the revival just a day away, we were encouraged on Sunday morning in church to attend the nightly services that were going to be held in the local theatre. While we were leery of the whole thing, Arlo and Linda asked us to go with them, and we agreed to go the first night. Right from the beginning my mental picture was shattered. The music was beautiful and I loved the incredible solos that were sung as well as the dueling pianos. The preaching was mesmerizing (even though I didn't quite "get it"), and so we faithfully left Sarah every night in the care of the provided child minders to attend. I think the music alone might even have been what drew me back night after night.

After every meeting, I would go back home feeling more confused than ever. Arlo and Linda came back home with us for coffee most nights, and they spent each of those late nights trying to help me figure out this whole thing called Faith. We'd battle back and forth on having to have a personal relationship with God.

Yet between the revival meetings and the talks with our good friends, it became more and more obvious that God did actually require a personal relationship with me. For some reason, I couldn't wrap my brain around that and it made me so angry! I must have heard that over and over in my life, so why couldn't I just accept it?

At the end of the week I was tired, frustrated, and I wanted to quit it all. But after the last night of the revival, Arlo and Linda stayed until the early hours of the morning, understanding my frustrations. Nothing seemed clearer to me than it did five nights earlier so I went to bed, disheartened.

I was lying there beside John, unable to sleep. It was well past 2 a.m. and John had no problem sleeping so I had no one to talk to. Thoughts kept going through my mind, but they only created more questions.

Finally I decided I had had enough and I told God so. (He was so prepared for that; I'm sure he was smiling at me...even encouraging me, holding his breath while I formed the words he'd been waiting so long to hear.) None too friendly or lovingly, I said to him, "Fine! If what you want is everything of me, then have it already! Take it all...whatever." Or something very similar to that.

Something very strange, okay, very God-like, happened at that split second. Instantly I felt a peace come over me, a quietness that surrounded me and a stillness within me. I knew that in my surrendering (albeit begrudgingly), it was exactly what God wanted. And required. There were no more questions at that moment and everything was absolutely right. At the same time as those feelings overtook me, as I was laying there in our darkened bedroom, I suddenly could see all of heaven rejoicing. It was like one huge party, with laughter, excitement, and incredible joy. There really are no words to describe it, but there was a sense of beautiful music, great brightness, and of hosts of angels just absolutely delighting in me!

In me!!

(In Luke 15:7 Jesus says, "I tell you that in the same way there will be more rejoicing in heaven over one sinner who repents than over ninety-nine righteous persons who do not need to repent.")

It was amazing.

I have no idea how long I saw that, but when it was all over, the most natural thing in the world to me was to beat on my poor unsuspecting and soundly sleeping husband. "John! John! You won't believe what just happened!" I just had to share it with him. I needed to tell him everything. I wish I could remember his reaction, but that is a complete blank to me. I'm guessing I just gushed it all out verbally and didn't even give him a chance to reply. Or perhaps the memory of what God had done for me that night overshadowed anything human.

That day my salvation was made complete. There was no more confusion about Faith and what it all meant. All was good.

Chapter 7

Good should never be confused with easy. Yet our lives were good. We had four healthy children, John had been promoted to manager of the credit union, and I was able to be a stay-at-home mom. Naturally there were bumps and bruises, but that's all par for the course when you are raising a family. Or married, for that matter.

One of the bumpy parts of our journey was in the area of schooling for our kids. For me personally, my dad's voice echoed in my head every time I thought about public versus Christian school. He used to say to me, regarding school, "Gerty, God is at the center of everything we do."

John and I both felt strongly that our children should be in a Christian school, but there wasn't one anywhere near us. A few people at that time were choosing to home-school their children, but they seemed pretty extreme to me. (You know, grinding their own wheat, churning their own butter and birthing their babies at home kind of extreme... "ew!") Consequently, our girls each began school in the local elementary school just a few blocks from our home.

We took an active role in the school. We attended every event, I served on the Parents Advisory Council, and we kept in close contact with each of the children's teachers. We even invited Sarah's kindergarten teacher to her sixth birthday party. (Nothing extreme or weird about that, is there?)

There were things in and about the school that we found difficult. Like the first year that Christmas was no longer celebrated in our school because it just wasn't politically correct to celebrate a religious holiday. Instead, the school held a Winter Solstice. To celebrate the solstice, the week before Christmas, a family talent show was held. In our attempt to bring Christ back into Christmas our family joined another young family in singing *Away in a Manger* as our part of the talent show.

Together our families sang the song while our youngest children, Brittany and Connor, both two years old, portrayed Mary and Joseph. They were dressed in character clothing and stood behind a cradle that held the baby Jesus. They were so adorable!

The song was going beautifully until one of the young couple took Jesus out of the cradle. Suddenly the other wanted the baby and a tug-of-war began. This went on for a few minutes until the one without the baby got in quite a huff, picked up the cradle and headed off the stage, followed, of course, by the irate holder of baby Jesus, now suddenly wanting the babe to have a nap.

I'm not so sure we got the message of Christmas across that night.

When Sarah was in grade three, Deborah in grade two, and Caitlin in kindergarten, the British Columbia Ministry of Education attempted a couple new ideas, one of them the Year 2000 Program. The program appeared to emphasize self-esteem, believing that children who felt good about themselves would strive to do better. As such, letter grades were no longer part of the primary grades and instead, teachers would focus on the attitude and effort.

Our little school had become a pilot school, and any new ideas that came from the Ministry were tried in our school first. Our students were guinea-pigged with some of the strangest ideas. Suddenly school seemed to become all about self-esteem and it appeared that academic accomplishment no longer seemed as important as how they felt about their learning.

As an example, Deborah came home with homework from her math class (grade two, remember). There were no numbers on the page, no mathematical questions. Instead there was a big box and in that box Deborah was to describe, through picture or word, how she felt about doing her math work.

We knew how she felt about it, and trust me, that would not have looked good on paper, whether picture or word. We couldn't help but wonder what her teacher would do if Deborah told her she hated it, would she then be exempt from the work? These papers were a regular part of the math program in grade two.

Another area of difficulty began the day Deborah came home and when I asked her what she had done in school that day, she said, "We did movies of the mind."

"Oh, really? Did you watch a movie?" I asked.

"No, we got to lay on the floor and close our eyes. And then Teacher turned off the lights and played pretty music."

Not at all sure of what might have gone on, I continued to probe. "Did you have a nap or just a quiet time?"

"Sort of, but Teacher told us to go to our special places inside us and find our special fairies that will help us."

Okay, I might have had a severely sheltered upbringing, but this sounded very much like the New Age practice of guided imagery. Alarm bells were going off for both John and I, and we asked the teacher if we could possibly sit in on one of those sessions. When we were repeatedly refused to be allowed to observe, those alarm bells turned into gongs.

By the end of that year we couldn't reconcile our value system to the school's, and we chose to take our kids out of the public school system and home-school them. It wasn't lost on me that I had just become one of those extreme people that I mentioned (minus the wheat, butter and home birthing). Although by then the home-schooling movement had grown in our area, and quite a few of our friends were trying it so it didn't seem as extreme as it did a few years earlier.

I have a photograph of the kids and myself on our first day home-schooling. The girls were entering grades four, three and one. Connor was almost three and just along for the ride. In the picture I was wearing a skirt and a blouse (as opposed to my usual jeans and t-shirt) and...is that makeup on my face? The girls were all wearing pretty dresses that I had made for them for their first day of school, and their hair was done in French braids or pony tails.

We were standing in front of the door to the official school room. The room used to be a nursery, then a music room, and now it became our school room. We had acquired four of the older style school desks, the ones where the seat is attached to the desk, and they were set up to face the front of the room where we had hung a large whiteboard. I had sewn a large eight-foot stuffed centipede/worm with paper clips attached to his feet and hung it from a ceiling beam above the kids' desks. His name was Waldo and the idea was that I would hang up the kids' art work and school papers from those little feet. (Didn't quite happen, but it's the thought that counts, right?)

We had always taken the first day of the school year as a seriously fun day, with new clothes, a special breakfast, a scavenger hunt, and fun snacks. Home-schooling was no different. Our first day of school at home was a fun day. There were, of course, brand new school supplies (that has always been, and might likely always be, the best part of school ever) and the usual scavenger hunt which sent the kids scattering all over the house in search of their personal school supplies. After organizing all their supplies in their desks, we did a craft, ate cream puffs, and that was our first day! No work, all play. Rather perfect, actually.

We all felt pretty good about our decision to home-school at that point.

In those early days of the schooling adventure we kept to a schedule each morning. At the beginning of each day I would read a devotional or a story followed by prayer. One morning, as usual, I asked the girls what they would like to pray for. Sarah started the requests.

"I'll pray for Tiffany." Tiffany was their former babysitter who was currently doing mission work in Romania.

"I'll pray for daddy at work," Deborah said.

Caitlin, not to be outdone by her sisters, but not having any ideas of her own, piped up with, "And I'll say Amen!!"

We knew that home-schooling was the right thing for our family at that time, and it was exciting to see the girls each learn at their own pace and in their own style. Naturally there were times of struggles with all of us being at home, difficulties with academics, and at times I wondered about my sanity (more than usual that is). I love change, you see. Not necessarily on a large scale, but I like to have variety in my days. When the same thing is expected of me on a daily basis I tend to get rebellious; I don't do predictability well.

As a result, we probably had more Pro-D days than normal. At one point I called them GOOMFASU days...Get Out Of My Face And Shut Up days... but then decided that was a little rude so we just went back to calling them Pro-D days. Yet even with the days off for good behaviour (anybody's, it didn't matter whose), we managed to keep up with all the academics. We all took the Reading, 'Riting and 'Rithmatic seriously. Or at least seriously enough to get through.

Because of my desire for constant change I also very much took the kids outside of the traditional learning box. Learning through living, in a way. For instance, when there was a spider in the house I would call the kids over. "Look at that beautiful spider God created. How many legs does he have? Isn't he interesting?" I'd give them 10 or 15 seconds to look (not too closely and only if it wasn't moving) before saying, "Now step on him for mommy, okay?" Catch the learning? They learned some science plus the fact that they didn't need to be afraid of those creepy, crawling, disgusting little critters (wish my mom had taught me that). And that they must never, under any circumstances, be allowed to live indoors with us.

Home-schooling had become more popular in the four years since our girls started school, and by the time we began there was a great community of families within 30 km of us, some real pioneers in the movement. As such, we joined together and had the usual field trips – fire hall, police station, museums, etc. There were sports days, Halloween celebrations, and monthly support meetings. We had our own Christmas concerts, back to school family wiener roasts, and year-end banquets.

We even went on weekend trips together to Fort Steele in the East Kootenays. Fort Steele sits on the western slopes of the Rocky Mountains and was a boom town during the 1864 Kootenay gold rush, but when the gold rush died and the town was bypassed, it became a ghost town. Since then it has been developed into a heritage town where you can walk the streets as it was in the nineteenth century.

For our weekend we all dressed in period costumes (jeans, cowboy hats, and boots for the guys, long dresses and bonnets for the girls) and experienced life like it was in the days of Sam Steele. (Sam Steele was part of the North West Mounted Police who was a peacemaker between the white people and the

Ktunaxa people during the gold rush years.) We cooked over wood fires, slept in the old barracks, and played cowboys and Indians (so politically incorrect now, but not so much then; there certainly was no disrespect meant).

Between our home-schooling community and our church, our kids never had a lack of socialization. They learned quickly to interact with others their own age, those younger, and most beautifully, those older. They benefited from meeting all different kinds of families and experiencing different customs and communities.

The girls were fairly easy to home-school; they were able to sit still, do their work, and be self-motivated. They had almost a natural desire to learn.

Connor, on the other hand, was not as interested in school work. Being a boy, he simply would not be confined to a desk. He would much rather play with his Lego, ride his bike outside, or just play in the dirt, and by the time he was in grade four, I realized that most of his learning had to wrapped up in something he could put his hands on.

That particular year we were following the government's outline for required learning, and one of his areas of study was the medieval times. He was more than interested in the castles, dragons, sword fighting, knights, and battles, but wasn't interested in answering questions or doing reports.

So I took him outside the box.

One of the learning outcomes expected was a story, and to make it more appealing to Connor I found a hardcover book with blank pages, just few enough to make it perfect for him to not just write a story, but an entire book. When he found out he could write and illustrate his own book about dragons, knights, and sword-fighting, he was all over it, and the result was a beautifully illustrated example of his learning.

To end off that particular unit with some deeper learning, the entire family participated in an authentic medieval meal that Connor planned and cooked almost completely by himself. He had to look up recipes, customs, and culture to make it real, while the rest of the family wore clothing appropriate to that time period. We all got into the spirit of the night, right down to not using plates, eating with our fingers, and throwing the bones on the floor.

My costume was that of a queen mother with a jewel encrusted crown made from an ice-cream bucket. The girls found long dresses and made pointy hats while John decked himself out as Robin Hood (I have to admit it was a great costume, but I look back and wonder why it did not seem strange that my husband was wearing tights...it just didn't...)

Home-schooling would end up being a successful eleven-year adventure for our family, not ending until the girls had finished their schooling (two of them eventually pursuing university degrees) and Connor halfway through grade seven.

Chapter 8

February was fast approaching, and that meant that Valentine's Day wasn't all that far off. We all loved Valentine's Day and were quite excited. I knew that it wouldn't be about John's and my romance, or about chocolate, roses, or a dinner out because we had long ago changed the focus of the day to being about the kids and our family.

I was excited for the day to begin, and as such I had hung up the Happy Valentine's Day banner the night before, blown up the red and white balloons, and pulled out the special tablecloth and placemats I had made for this day.

The energy level was high the next day as all the kids knew what would be happening. Sure enough, the heart-shaped cookies came out for a snack and shortly thereafter there was a knock on the door. All four of the kids ran to answer it.

The door opened to a flower delivery person who had her arms full with five wrapped bundles. The kids eagerly peeked in each package to find an envelope with their name on it. The flowers had become a tradition from their dad; each of them received a different coloured carnation, and I received a single rose. It always made me smile to see how getting one single flower delivered for each of the kids specifically from their dad made them feel so special.

But the biggest event of the day was still to come.

The celebration meal.

Weeks earlier each of the kids had invited one friend to join them in their Valentine's Day dinner, with the instructions that everyone invited was to be dressed up (shirts and ties for any boys and dresses for the girls) and expected to be on their best behaviour. They had no idea what exactly the evening would hold for them, but they were as excited about it as we were.

Before the guests arrived, John and I quasi-renovated the kitchen and dining area of our house. We moved the dining room table into the open area away from the kitchen and set it up as a restaurant with the red tablecloth, good china, wineglasses, and candles.

This year's restaurant was called Chez Gertrude; our kitchen and dining room transformed into a place to experience French cuisine.

As the guests came to Chez Gertude, John, playing the role of waiter, greeted them at the door.

"Bonjour, mademoiselle, monsieur. Bienvenue!"

Naturally the response was just a giggle, no words, as they had no idea what was just said or how they should respond.

John took their jackets, seated them at the table, and gave them menus. The menus had been painstakingly made by us and included appetizers such as Snail Liver Pate and Peu de Pizza a la Pepperone. Main course choices were Poulet Pot Pie, Maison de Tacos, and Perfecta Pasta. For dessert we offered Crème de Ice avec Jello and Chez Gertrude Mousse. The drinks menu included Eau de Moo, Plain Eau, Framboise Rouge, and Café au Lait.

While John was the formal waiter every year, I was the crazy cook. Every year. We always bantered back and forth in a weird mix of English and whatever language went with the restaurant's theme. While this year's theme was French, neither of us was bilingual, although we did both have a smattering of high school French. We made a rather pitiful attempt to put that to good use, inventing words if we needed to. Of course everything we said in the kitchen we said loud enough for the kids to hear.

"Qu'est-ce que la beverage?" John asked each guest after they'd had a few moments to look at the menu. By then the kids were into the evening a bit and would venture to pronounce the items on the menu. If they would pronounce it wrong, they would very likely get an earful of muttered French/English about their lack of language skills.

After getting all their orders, John thanked them and politely took a step away from the table. He then turned towards the kitchen and yelled at me, "Un Eau de Moo, trois Framboise Rouge et deux Café au Lait! Oh, and deux plain eau!"

"Oui, oui," I answered, as that was almost the extent of my French.

John served the drinks and then took their dinner orders in the same fashion as he did the drinks. Again, he yelled them out at me, causing the kids to be in hysterics.

"Ah, fermez la bouche!" I yelled back. I grumbled and complained in my pretend French. (Hey, I hated that class, skipped as much as I could, so what else could I do but pretend?) As I was cooking, I banged the pots and pans around for effect.

"Ah, ze chef, a leetle beet, how you say, crazy, a la tete?" John said to the kids as he rolled his eyes and drew circles in the air beside his head. "Eegnore ze crazy lady, yes?"

The children and their friends laughed until their sides ached, but quickly joined in by asking for more drinks, even complaining about their food. Anything they could think of to prolong the evening.

The kids loved those nights, and truth be told, so did we. Through those evenings once a year we were able to show the kids how much we loved them, but we were also able to teach them what proper manners were. ("You, garcon," John would say, "Ze napkin, it goes on ze lap, yes? S'il vous plait, mademoiselle, you close ze lips when you chew ze food, yes?")

These family events created a foundation that would serve the kids and I well when our "perfect" world would come crashing down.

Chapter 9

So there we were, married for 10 years, a family of six. While I had been journaling up to then, most entries were about my pregnancies and then the milestones in the kids' lives. It seemed like around the 10 year mark, I began to look at things a little deeper.

May, 1991 journal entry: *Spiritually things could not be better. John and I are "growing" together – it's wonderful. We had our 10ᵗʰ anniversary and we both feel like we have come a long way and will continue to grow... We are truly more in love with each other now and at such a deep level.*

June 7, 1991 journal entry: *If I could pass on one thing to each of you [children], it would be my desire for you to come to know Jesus as your Saviour. Only in Him is there any hope in this scary, sometimes horrid world. If any of you are at all like me, your Opa, and your Great-Opa, you will ask, "Why does God..." many times in your lives. At times you simply will lash out in anger or sadness and scream at Him. That's okay – He can take it. He loves you, each of you. He doesn't mind your questions. Just give Him time to answer them, and remember that He's the only one with the answers. He does not make mistakes, He works everything to the good, and He will never leave you.*

In addition to being a family, John's and my relationship was doing well. As in any family, our children unintentionally added the usual stress. In our case, all you have to do is look at the numbers, and if you've had children, or even just been around them for any period of time, you'll understand. (Four kids in six years, need I say more?) Add into that our home-schooling and being around each other 24 hours a day, seven days a week, and you have a recipe for stress.

Nonetheless, we got through times that were discouraging and sometimes even ugly. Our 7th anniversary and the year leading up to it were especially difficult for me. That was the year after I'd had Caitlin, our third child. She was the easiest baby to have around, always happy. But even that didn't make up for the simple fact that I had three children, aged three and under, all in some stage of cloth diapers. The demands on me made it a tough year. Along with being a full-time mom I also had to be a wife. I do not blame John for wanting a wife, but my reality was a little overwhelming for me. All day I wiped bums, cooked food, did laundry, and cleaned up…okay, maybe I didn't actually do the clean up, but I knew I should, so then I'd feel guilty…

When John came home from work, we'd all sit down and have dinner together before another round of work…dishes (no dishwasher, I might add), bath time, story time, bed time.

Then came our own bed time, and good night! The man wanted sex. Did he not understand that that caused those three children? Who would want to keep doing that, I ask you?

Well, it wasn't me that was for sure.

It's not that I hated sex. On the contrary, I enjoyed the closeness and there were times it was great, but it just wasn't something I went out of my way to do too often (you know, like shopping for example). I felt bad for John, and I really tried hard to change, but I felt like I could never measure up to what he wanted.

We fought about it, but I don't think either of us knew what we were actually fighting about (I was simply exhausted; he simply wanted sex; neither of us even attempted to understand the problem from the other's perspective).

That year in particular seemed like I was always being pulled in one direction or another with no time for myself.

Just before our 7th anniversary John took Sarah, then four years old, to Edmonton to celebrate his grandparents' 55th anniversary. I spent many hours, while he was away, wondering what the future held for us, how I would get past what felt like such a difficult time.

John knew it wasn't easy for me. He was very patient with me to a point, but we both felt far apart from the other, not really understanding where the other was coming from.

When John and Sarah came back from their trip John surprised me by giving me two gifts to celebrate our anniversary.

The first was a gold wedding band. I was thrilled that he had remembered that I wanted a simple band to wear without my engagement ring. In the old Dutch tradition when you were engaged you wore a gold band on your left hand, and when you were married you moved the ring from your left hand to your right hand. I had always loved that tradition and wanted to carry it on, putting a gold band on my right hand when we got engaged and then moving it to my left during our marriage ceremony. When John and I got engaged, he wasn't so enamored of the idea and insisted on buying me an engagement ring and then a wedding band with a diamond in it to match. (I think he felt that going with just the band might make him look cheap, not Dutch...or is that redundant?) Deep in my heart, however, I always wished for a plain gold band like my parents and their parents.

The timing for this gift from John was so perfect. Not just because he had remembered something that was important to me, but because it made me think about our wedding vows and our marriage, realizing that we had committed to each other seven years previously, and we'd stay committed. It was really that simple.

Good thing I opened that gift first, I tell you, because the second gift that John brought home for me was lingerie. It was beautiful and even somewhat practical: a white satin and lace teddy. While I could see the beauty of it, I couldn't help but wonder what that man of mine was thinking. Did he think that if only I had some sexy new clingy lingerie to put on the body that had birthed three kids in three years I would want to make wild passionate love with him? That it was simply a lack of slink and lace (now there's a name for a lingerie shop) that kept me aloof sexually?

I put on my new wedding band.

Oh how I wanted to be what John needed, and I knew what he needed was not out of the ordinary (women talk). I knew it was me. I remember one day when a girlfriend was talking about lying in bed with her husband naked, just talking.

Huh? Naked? Talking? Ew! It seriously blew my mind then that people would do that.

Yet in spite of my weird thinking, there was so much that was good about our relationship and all that was good kept us committed to each other. Every morning we still got up together and shared a cup of tea (even when we had four children, although by then it had changed to coffee). We still started and ended each day together, never going to bed without the other. John called me at least two or three times a day from work just to see how we all were. He'd always be the one I would call when something would come up or I'd need to talk, and most days he still came home to have lunch with us.

We shared everything. We lived as if there were no secrets between us; I kept nothing from him. Best friends, remember?

As ridiculous as it might sound, we honestly agreed on child rearing, discipline, God and our faith, finances (as much as talked about it, we agreed), our future. We enjoyed each other's company immensely and loved to do spontaneous things together. If one of us had an idea, more often than not, the other one would think it was great, and we'd go right then and there to do it. Whether it was making our own concrete paving blocks for a walkway, tobogganing at midnight in our pyjamas, or...

It was a snowy day in December (they all were) and we were putting up our Christmas tree. The post and beam style of our home, the loft, and high ceilings lent itself to some serious Christmas decorating. We had huge windows in the living room, and there was always a winter scene when we put up the tree. Always.

At that time of our lives, I was into doing themes at Christmas. From primary colours and paper cut-outs (you had to be there) to naked trees (deciduous, naked, whatever) and white lights (which eventually became a popular look, but it sure wasn't back then), we did it.

This particular year I had decided to do the tree in navy blue and gold.

It was 9 p.m. when the six of us finished decorating our tree, and it looked spectacular with mini white lights, gold beads, gold and navy balls, and navy ribbons. Standing back and gazing at it, I declared that our tree topper was just not right. Right there and then I decided we just had to find a better one, and so we piled all four of the kids in the car and drove an hour across the border into the United States where there was a Wal-Mart open until midnight (this was before there were any Wal-Marts in Canada).

All we found was a bigger blue ribbon, but we created a family memory that exists to this day.

One year we had three trees that John put together on a base. They were again naked, but with the three combined they looked fantastic with the high ceilings and windows. After Christmas, I still thought they were so beautiful and they triggered another spontaneous moment.

I decided to take off the Christmas decorations but leave on the lights and keep the trees. I had grand plans to decorate them differently each month with the kids. For January the kids and I made hundreds of paper snowflakes; February were red hearts; March's tree was shamrock-laden. April might have been raindrops. It was while I was cutting out and colouring what seemed like hundreds of paper daisies for our May trees that I got tired. Really tired. As I wondered what on earth I was doing, the proverbial light went on...

...and the trees came down.

I even let John...oh, are you ready for this?...perm my hair. I don't know whose idea it was, and I don't know what we were thinking, but someone should definitely have stopped us. He had had his own hair permed in the eighties and he once permed his cousin's hair, so it seemed like a great idea.

It wasn't.

The result of that spontaneity was a mad scramble at 4:30 p.m. on a Saturday to find a hair dresser that could fix my hair. I found myself going from hair salon to hair salon begging for a hair cut. I finally found one willing to tackle my frizzy, kinky, burned head of hair, but I didn't come out of that salon without a severe tongue lashing about home perms. (I didn't have the heart to tell them that it was my husband that I had allowed to do that to me.)

It wasn't until we were married for 14 years that we took our first real vacation alone since having children. We went to Hawaii for a week. Even though it wasn't my ideal vacation spot (not much liking the hot sun or putting on a bathing suit), I was more than ecstatic to go on a holiday alone with my husband, the person that I enjoyed being with more than any other.

While there we took surfing lessons and went snorkeling. The surfing was fun, learning the ropes on dry land and then being set loose into the waves. I can't say that either of us was any good at it, but we definitely had fun.

On another day we rented a vehicle and drove to a beach that was known for its snorkelling. I had never snorkelled before, but I did think that fish were beautiful. With all the different kinds and colours, swimming among them could only be fun.

We rented all our gear, bought bags of fish food, and waded into the gorgeous clear blue ocean. John took to it like the proverbial fish to water.

I was a little more hesitant to get into the water. You see, I love water in any form, whether it be a stream, creek, lake, river, waterfall, or ocean, but more as an observer. I'm happier to sit on the beach (in the shade) than to frolic in the waves. Consequently I took my time getting into the ocean, enjoying just being there, observing the fish swimming, taking it all in. After a few minutes I immersed myself in the water and prepared to meet the fish.

They were quite ready to meet me as well, and before I knew it I had come face to face with my first fish. And I do mean face to face; we're talking eye contact here. Then along came another. And another. Soon they were inviting all their friends (I could see their lips moving and it looked like they were saying, "hey, guys, we got a live one here, come over and help us torment her!") Yes they were pretty, but they just kept wiggling all around me and touching me!

I freaked out and was almost in tears, frantic to get away from the masses of squirming, swimming, touching creatures. Do you have any idea how hard it is to run out of a deep body of water when wearing flippers?...while in panic mode?

When I finally made my way back to the beach I gladly took off my snorkeling gear and put it and my unused fish food on the sand before lying down on my towel. Trying to get my heart rate back down and salvage a beach day, I closed my eyes and prepared to relax.

I let the sun warm my skin and began to put the entire awful fish-swarming incident out of my mind.

Suddenly it cooled down and the sun seemed to disappear. I felt a strange breeze and, even stranger, I heard a quiet noise begin and then grow louder, "whoosh whoosh whoosh." Slowly I opened my eyes to check to see if the sun would be coming back soon or if we were in for a cloudy afternoon. I expected to see a blue sky with some fluffy clouds moving on their way by. Instead, I opened my eyes and thought at first that the demon fish had sprouted wings to haunt me. Then I realized it was a multitude of flapping wings and a mass of moving bodies hovering just above me and beside me! Mere inches from my face a flock of birds was dive-bombing my fish food, leading me into another frenzy of panic.

From frantic fish to crazy birds, that beach day was not one of the highlights of our trip for me, but it did leave me with a memory that I could eventually laugh about.

Something else happened on this trip that seemed quite normal at the time, but later haunted me a little. It was another of our spontaneous moments, but definitely the strangest one yet. We were walking downtown, and as we passed a jewelry store John suggested that we get our ears pierced together.

Yes, for some reason it seemed normal to me that my husband would suggest we get our ears pierced. This was strange, considering that this was in the time when I didn't know any man, boy, or male teenager that had a pierced ear.

I already had two piercings in both ears, so John suggested that I get another hole in one ear and he'd get one of his ears pierced (that cheap Dutch gene coming out; we could get both done on one bill). We were on holidays, and it was something that appealed to my slightly rebellious side, so I eagerly went along with the idea. We each got our ear pierced with a tiny diamond stud.

I wasn't so sure it was a good idea any more when we got back home and my mom saw his earring for the first time. She was standing at the door to the basement and John was standing at the door to the upstairs. They were side by side when she noticed it. She stopped, stared, and said what I think was the first thing that came to her mind. "What?! I hope that doesn't mean you're gay or anything."

From then on, that comment haunted me a little and John's earring bothered me a bit because I was afraid people might think he was gay.

While we most definitely had great times and our life was a happy one, we also had our share of disagreements. I think the more accurate term would be fights. I know I threw at least one apple and one bran muffin. (In hindsight, I really shouldn't have buttered it; it left a grease mark on the wall that I never could get off.) We were not good at conflict resolution; we brought everything into a fight. From our first disagreement ever to mother-in-laws and character flaws, it was all pretty much fair game.

Yet even with those normal hiccups I knew that, bottom line, we had what it took to go the distance.

And I had the wedding band to remind me.

Chapter 10

After years of being our best friends, Arlo and Linda had moved away, leaving a huge gap in our lives. Over the years Linda and I had become fast friends. We had spent so many hours and days together, both of us choosing to stay at home with our children, sharing the same values and dreams. We visited with each other all the time, went shopping together, took our kids to the church's Moms and Tots program, and challenged each other to grow in our faith.

I felt lost when she moved away.

Linda wasn't my only friend, but she was my best friend and the only one that lived close by. All of our other friends lived about 30 km away. Our church was the half way point between us with very few people choosing to live on our half. For a time it was lonely for me; it was a long drive with kids to visit other friends and even a phone call was long distance and could get costly. (That was in the time when the only way you could make a cheap long-distance phone call was to call after 11 p.m. and before 8 a.m. Daytime calls were always regular rates.)

A year and a half after Arlo and Linda's move, a new family moved into town, Joe and Joanne. Joanne and I hit it off immediately, which was surprising seeing as we were such opposites. She was petite, I was not. She was educated, I was, well, sort of. She appeared to have lots of money, I had way less. You get the picture.

But Joanne was and still is the most gracious and soft-spoken woman I know, an incredible hostess, an amazing teacher, and a dedicated shopper. The first time we met them,

they invited us over for lunch after church "for some leftovers."
Her leftovers were better than anything I'd ever cooked and the
friendship began. For all four of us, but mostly between Joanne
and I.

It wasn't long before I realized that I had found my new best
friend.

While Joanne brought a sense of culture and stability to my
life, it wasn't all one-sided by any means. I brought to her life the
impulsiveness and wild side that she, being an only child and
always having been such a good girl, seemed to lack. Her idea of
a great time was to shop; my idea was to do it at midnight. In
Spokane (250 km away).

She and Joe and their two children also attended our church
and were quickly welcomed into the group of friends already
established there. Joanne and I began doing many things
together: Moms and Tots, singing duets in church, planning
parties, and sharing meals.

Before long, Joanne brought one of her neighbours into our
friendship, Beverley. Bev was in the same stage of her life as
Joanne and I with young children and babies. The three of us
formed an immediate bond and it wasn't long before we were
sharing everything, from coffee times, recipes, and baby stories
to weekend shopping trips (in Spokane, of course). On those
weekends we would leave all our children with our husbands to
drive a few hours away and spend some time together, shopping,
eating, and laughing.

It was on one of those trips that one of us suggested we get
ourselves some false nails. This was before the gel nail era. And
not salon nails, either. No, no, no, I'm talking the plastic ones in
a package that come with their own glue. Much like crazy glue as
it turned out. It seemed like such a great idea that we
immediately went off to do some midnight shopping.

Those nails were not really one of our best ideas. Not one of us was familiar with the false nails scene and I'm guessing we, or at the very least one of us, should have read the fine print on the directions (oh, I just know what you are thinking...shades of wallpapering...yes, I was still not reading directions). Perhaps it was because we never read the fine print that we found ourselves glued to our pajamas, to the table, to each other. Seriously glued. In fact, after only a couple nails, both Bev and I came unglued (pun totally intended) and gave up. Joanne insisted on finishing hers, and so we spent the remainder of our evening sipping wine and laughing at Joanne's determination to put on ten rather long, new nails and then paint them bright red. They could not have been longer or brighter.

You have to understand something about Joanne here. She is one well put together lady. Her hair is always neat, her lipstick is always on, and her handbag, not to be mistaken for a purse, always matched her shoes. She was not one to follow trends; she was simply that classy.

Those long bright red nails said a lot, but "classy" was not it.

We arrived home late the next night, and it wasn't until the following morning in church when Joanne was at the piano that she was faced with the consequences of her persistence. Two things happened. Firstly, she discovered that playing piano with half-inch extensions on her fingers wasn't quite the same as playing with her usual short stubbies, and secondly, her husband suddenly noticed her nails. Yeah, I know....where was he the night before, and how could he not have noticed them before church? Well, my answer to that is that Joe is a man. As in one of those "real men" (the term redneck comes to mind)...that really does explain it all.

Joe was so unimpressed that his first reaction was to compare his dear, sweet, gentle, and classy wife to, how shall I say this...a lady of the evening. Yes, that's pretty much what those nails screamed, but we weren't going to tell her that. We could always count on Joe to say things that no one else would.

Suffice to say they came off that very afternoon and took just about as much time and persistence to remove as they did to put on. Not as much fun without Bev and I, though.

I guess the three of us weren't always the best influence on each other on these shopping trips, because none of us ever really questioned the others' ideas. It was like we were teenagers again. When one of us suggested laser tag as a lark, which had yet to come to our part of the world, we did it. (I cried there too, being so easily spooked in the dark, not to mention being shot at!)

When it was suggested that we surprise our husbands with strategically placed rose tattoos (the temporary kind, of course), we went midnight shopping again. Fortunately there was no glue required for the application, so the tattoos were much less traumatic than the nails and a little more welcomed when we got home.

It was all harmless. And so when the idea of stopping at a casino on the way to Spokane came up there was really no real reason to say no.

It was my first trip into a casino and when I stepped into this place with all the noise and cigarette smoke I felt like I'd crossed over onto the highway to hell. A bit extreme maybe, but the whole place hit me as such a place of desperation. It appeared that the people there were consumed with winning, as if their lives depended on it, and I felt so sad for them. I didn't want to put a damper on our trip, however, so I said nothing and we stayed. We set ourselves a limit to spend on the slot machines, something like five dollars, and when that was gone we left.

It wasn't fun for me at all.

Perhaps the strong emotion made me feel like I had done something wrong because I didn't share this little excursion with John. It was the only secret I ever kept from him.

Joanne, Bev, and I were quite the Suzy Homemakers (Suzy was the predecessor to Martha Stewart). A different time and a different place, and we could have been The Three Marthateers. We had some serious skills, and for several years we put them together and set up tables at the 'Christmas Fair' in the local hotel. We made and sold fancy pastries, peanut brittle, chocolate truffles, and assorted Christmas baking. Our signature was our red blouses and white eyelet aprons which, of course, we had made ourselves.

Every birthday and every Christmas we would use to celebrate our friendship together. For one of my birthdays Bev and Joanne picked up Chinese food and a bottle of wine and kidnapped me. We went to the drive-in theatre where we laid in the back of the truck and watched the movie while we ate our dinner.

Each celebration was different, but they were never short on fun.

Because John and I didn't have any family near us, all our friends became very important to us; more like extended family than friends. We regularly visited with each other and shared occasions. Very few of our friends had family in the area so we created that for each other. Occasions like Thanksgiving, Christmas, and Easter became ones where we'd all get together to celebrate. We'd have wiener roasts on long weekends, toboggan in the winter, and go to each other's homes after church on Sundays.

With them we created a social club within our church and called it TNT (Twenties N' Thirties) – fun nights for young couples. We would get together one Saturday night a month, participating in various activities. I remember one particularly disastrous night when one couple planned an entire evening and called it "games your mother never taught you." One of these games was played in the dark in a very small room in the highest part of the house...people crawling around on their hands and knees...accidental groping...some screaming...yes, me...and, well, the whole evening didn't go over well...I know why my mother never taught me any of those games. The only thing good that came from that evening was that we laughed about it for years afterwards.

Our church was growing and changing. One of those changes was a new youth pastor, Rick Zufelt. He was single, skinny, and in his twenties so our TNT group adopted him. Although it wasn't said out loud, I think all of us women made it our mission to find him a wife and fatten him up (misery loves company and all).

John and I invited Rick over for dinner quite regularly. I have to say that I felt somewhat sorry for him, as most of his meals were either hot dogs or ravioli from a can, so it was nice to cook him dinner. In visiting with him, he became a special friend to our whole family. Rick had a flare for writing and drama, and it wasn't long before he worked himself into a routine at our place; one I'm sure he developed to get out of helping with the dishes. After dinner, John and I would begin to clear off the dirty plates and get ready to wash them when Rick and all our kids would disappear into the living room. While we were left doing the dishes, Rick would sit on the couch surrounded by all four of our kids and read stories with great expression and using weird voices.

Rick was passionate about God and about youth; he took them to the most amazing places spiritually; there were no youth that he left untouched in his ministry. Rick also used his gift for drama, both writing and acting in Easter dramas that he put on at the church for the community. He moved people in the audience to think about Christ and what He'd done for them. Because of our friendship, we joined him wholeheartedly for those dramas, whether it was helping with the coffee house in the church basement after the performances or actually being in the performances ourselves. One particular year Rick somehow managed to talk Deborah and I, Deborah just ten years old at the time, into performing as main characters in one of his dramas.

Our group of friends constantly challenged both John and I to grow spiritually. Because of our traditional and conservative upbringing and church, we were reluctant to change. That old expression "if something ain't broke, don't fix it" often applied to our faith. I had an excellent foundation of faith from my parents, and it was that foundation that led me closer and closer to God. Yet I was hesitant to let go of some beliefs as an adult, and when I was questioned about certain convictions that I held I really had no answer except for "because that's just the way it is." Our friends would challenge that thinking. Not with the intent to change me or to make me believe in something different, but more to understand why I held certain thoughts and to challenge me to know why.

One of those areas was that of baptism, and as the years passed we became more and more convinced that we needed to be baptized. Everything that we read in the Bible regarding baptism seemed to call us to have an outward showing of what was happening inwardly. We talked to pastors and friends (on both sides of the issue), read everything we could about it, and were finally personally convinced that it was a step of obedience we just had to do. It wasn't an easy decision, but it was the right one for us.

One Sunday night in January John and I put on the traditional long gowns of baptism. I was the first to walk down the steps into the baptismal tank after Clayton, the senior pastor and also a close friend.

I shared my testimony, my journey of faith and how it led me to that moment. Then I lifted my arms across my chest and Clayton gently put me under the water and then brought me back up. It was like a load was lifted off me. I don't believe anything happened to me as far as my salvation goes, but there was a sense of peace about having taken another step in my faith.

Shortly after I came up from the water, and before John was to come down the steps, Clayton got a nosebleed. When it didn't stop, it was decided to have Rick baptize John.

Unfortunately, Rick did not come prepared to do any baptizing and was wearing a suit and tie. While we were all in the church basement trying to figure out what Rick could wear under his own pastoral baptismal gown, I suggested he wear my pants. Yes, my pants. They were black stretch pants (sort of like tights, but not quite so, well, tight!). With stirrups. Highly fashionable for the time.

Rick might have been a pastor, but he was a bit of a redneck (Alberta roots, what can I say) so the thought of wearing my pants was abhorrent to him. Nonetheless, he was also one of the most modest and frugal people I'd ever met, so when he was left with the choice of either wearing only his underwear under that robe (a light-coloured robe that he knew would cling to him when he got out of the water), thus saving a dry cleaning bill, or wearing my pants and living with that humiliation, he chose my pants.

Having Rick baptize John was incredibly meaningful to us as he had become a close friend to both of us.

Perhaps to avoid any more of our meddling, Rick eventually found a woman to spend the rest of his life with (without us...go figure!). He began, innocently, to write to Tiffany, the young woman who used to baby-sit for us and was now doing missions work in Romania (the same Tiffany that the girls prayed for every morning). Their correspondence led to a romance which led to a wedding.

Both John and I were thrilled and honoured when these two special people asked John to be the Master of Ceremonies at their wedding.

Rick was a great influence in John's life, but as things unfolded it wouldn't be enough.

Chapter 11

It was 1996 and John was looking for a new job and a move, regularly applying for management positions in credit unions across the province. For one reason or another no job offers materialized.

April 30, 1996 journal entry: *John is restless in his job...I think he may be feeling the start of that age – a mild midlife crisis? Maybe this restlessness is the Lord's prompting for something else.*

Shortly after our baptism, John became an elder in our church, and around the time of his restlessness our church brought in a speaker for a week of revival meetings. It was on a much smaller scale than the one we had attended years earlier; the meetings were held in our church rather than the theatre each night and were of a more personal nature, more aimed at challenging us all in our faith. Again John and I attended each night and we felt our faith deepen.

It wasn't as earth-shattering for me as the revival that brought me into a personal relationship with God; it quite simply brought me to a new level of faith. I was challenged to get up early each morning to pray and read my Bible. Early meant 6 a.m.

Problem was I still hated mornings.

Until then the only reason I would even consider getting up at that time of night (I don't care what you call it, 6 a.m. is and always will be night to me) was if a baby was crying and needed nursing.

Nonetheless, it was clear to me that God knew what He wanted from me (while having the last laugh over the morning part), and I knew what I needed to do. And so I began getting up at 6 a.m. to meet with Him. I would stagger into another room and curl up in a chair to read my bible and pray. John was also challenged to begin devotions and would go upstairs into the loft for his personal time with God.

May 11 journal entry: *Six a.m. I'm up willingly, well-rested, refreshed and called to pray!*
May 12: *Six a.m. Here again.*
May 13: *A little tough to wake up and get into prayer.*

Within four days the novelty of my "calling" had already begun to wear off and the discipline had to kick in. The impulsive part of me wanted an instant easy time each morning, desiring a fresh and wakeful attitude (years later that has yet to happen, truth be told, but I'm not giving up hope) and a good connection with God. I did not quit, however. I persevered. I was determined to do my part in furthering my relationship with God, and if all I did was get up in obedience to read my bible and pray, I knew that would be enough. God himself would take care of the connection and depth. I was encouraged knowing that John was also praying and reading his bible right above me in our loft.

Only a few mornings later, John had an experience that I personally believe was a turning point in his life, although neither of us knew it at that time and it would be years before I would look back on that experience as what I would call his AHA! moment. I described it in my journal entry of that day.

May 15: *I am so discouraged this morning. In my prayer time I only hit the ceiling. I tried clearing out each and every thing that could stand in my way to God, but I couldn't concentrate; I didn't feel connected whatsoever....*

Then John told me later that he'd had the most incredible experience in his devotions. He was having his time of praise and he felt God saying, "Be still and know that I am God." He did just that and felt that he was completely in the presence of God, communing with Him (John's words). As a result of the revival, for the first time in our marriage I saw John spend time alone with God. We were not praying together as a husband and wife, but individually we were both looking to deepen our relationship with God.

It felt so good.

In the midst of this incredible time in our marriage, when we were both so right with God, we had our 15th anniversary. John surprised me with a four-day trip without the kids.

May 18, 1996 journal entry: *I am sitting up in bed looking out the wall of windows and French doors and watching the ocean. We are in Cannon Beach, Oregon, in the same place where we stayed 15 years ago on our honeymoon...*

On our way we stopped at a jewelry store....John bought me a gold cross on a delicate gold chain...

...we walked onto the outside deck of our room and admired the beach. When I came back I noticed a vase full of yellow roses. There were 15, one for each year we've been married. Then John handed me a gift. In it were a pair of diamond stud earrings to match the little one we got in Hawaii...they are stunning! I was absolutely shocked at how romantic it all was. The huge bathroom has a heart shaped Jacuzzi tub and did I mention the fireplace in the living room and the king size bed?...

We had reservations for dinner...truly the most remarkable meal...we brought back memories and we talked of the past 15 years, how we've grown and changed and need to continue to do so. We see this point as such a moving forward place because we are both so right with God now...after dinner we went barefoot down to the water. What began as a walk turned into a run, holding hands, into the water, laughing and screaming. It was cold, and it didn't take long to freeze our feet and ankles enough to turn around and come out again. It was wild.

...after church (in a lighthouse!) we went for brunch...John told me of his little secret he's been hanging onto since this past October. He has said that when I get my grade ten piano he will buy me a grand piano. So last October when he saw that I was serious about my piano, he borrowed several thousand dollars to begin financing it (he never told me)...I have very little problem with the loan but I am somewhat concerned that John is so easily able to keep secrets from me...

...This weekend has been so perfect it almost is too difficult to put on paper. We have walked, talked, relaxed, and thoroughly enjoyed each other's company. We have recaptured the laughter and love of our courtship days. As sad as it is to leave behind, it was the best holiday I've ever had; I wouldn't change a word, a moment, anything. I am thoroughly grateful to have had these past four days.

That four-day escape was to be our last holiday for just the two of us. I believe it was an effort on John's part to really make our marriage work for him.

Back home I continued to get up most mornings at 6 a.m.

July 4, 1996 journal entry: *Lord, I recognize how badly I need to be with you each day, but I need your help in getting up each morning at six. I love the idea that your face is the first I see each day, but I am lazy. I crave sleep and desire to be rested. So, Lord, wake me up tomorrow at six, refreshed and eager to meet with you.*

Lord, I get so excited about what you can do through me. I believe absolutely in your power and your provision of prayer. Help me to tap into you fully every moment....There are endless requests I have for myself. I long for confidence in the person you made me. I desire to be confident in you, not in others around me. Lord, please give me that confidence...I think of John. I desire your will for his life. Thank you for his desire for you, strengthen him in that daily walk. Give him peace at work, happiness in his day, joy in what he does...I pray for our family, that we may bond together to be a happy family, a complete family in your love, with you at the center. Help us to focus on you.

As 1996 came to a close, we appeared to be at a turning point. I have a picture of Joanne, Bev, and me that was taken in December of that year. We were celebrating Christmas and Joanne's birthday over dinner in a restaurant, smiling at the camera. It's a memorable picture in hindsight because within the next year, Joanne would undergo major surgery and turn 40, Bev's marriage would end, and I would be moving away.

Even the restaurant would burn down.

Chapter 12

John's restlessness that I noticed the year previously worsened. By then he had been working at the credit union for 16 years, and in that time had earned his CGA degree. It seemed very natural that he wanted a change, not surprising that he'd want to move up the ladder. After all the resumes he'd been sending out it didn't come as a surprise when he finally got a job offer from the credit union in Enderby, B.C.

I had never heard of Enderby which apparently wasn't that unusual for anyone who didn't actually live there. John knew next to nothing about it either, and so we decided to go and check it out before making any decisions. Naturally we would take all four of our kids with us. After all, this decision would affect their lives, too.

Our first visit to the little city (population approximately 3,500) to see what it was like and to look for housing was not all that great. As we drove down the road, coming into the city, the first smell we had was of cows, and one of our kids exclaimed, "Ew!! It smells like Chilliwack!" (Chilliwack was the city where John and I grew up - the "cow belt" of B.C. which is naturally quite cow-smellish.)

That weekend actually turned out to be less than not all that great; more like one from hell. The room we had reserved was given to someone else and while we were there, the local river flooded which meant that the city water became muddy. It was like one of the plagues in Exodus, I tell you.

Eventually we were given the hotel's "penthouse" in lieu of our reserved room, which was only called such because it had separate bedrooms and a kitchen. It wasn't like it had a Jacuzzi tub, walls of windows with views or king size beds or any of the amenities one would expect from a penthouse suite. John and I, in fact, slept on a hide-a-bed in the living room. Unfortunately, it was directly over the bar where country music ruled. At that time, we were not so fond of country music and most certainly not through the floor boards under our bed. The hoots and hollers and the rhythmic stomping of the line-dancing crowd didn't do much for us, either.

Because of the flooding, when we turned the tap on to make tea, brown ooze came out. Taking a shower was out and brushing our teeth had to be done with bought water (in the time before bottled water was normal).

That Saturday all six of us plus a real estate agent went in and out of fourteen houses hoping to find one that we would fall in love with. Not one of them really grabbed us the "the one."

All in all the weekend was a bust.

It was on the drive out of town that I kind of hissed at John (I always presumed hissing was always out of the hearing range of children – I might have been wrong on that). "Please. Do. Not. Make. Me. Move. To. That. Hell. Hole." I couldn't see anything good there.

God did.

John didn't have to make me; together we chose to move to Enderby. We both believed that this was God's choice for us. It wasn't an easy decision for John and I and not an easy concept for any of us, leaving everything we knew in Rossland. Our kids were at that time 13, 11, 10 and 6.

July 29, 1997 journal entry: *We're moving. After 16 and a half years, our entire married life and the only place our kids have ever known. We'll be leaving the birthplace of our kids, the church where we were baptized, the only friends we've made as a couple or as a family, all the areas that hold memories for us as a family. Where will life take us now? Will we make friends as easily, will we fit in, find a place of comfort?*

The only thing we knew for sure about Enderby, and the one thing that made us feel connected, was that there was a great little church there, the Enderby Evangelical Chapel. The directors and cabin leaders of the summer bible camp that our girls had gone to, all of whom we highly regarded, had grown up in this church. Besides being confident that God was directing our future, we were also confident there was a strong place to worship and warm people to welcome us.

The last days of our life in Rossland were difficult as we packed everything up, tried to help the kids deal with the move, and said goodbye to those we loved so dearly.

The night before we left, the eve of my 37th birthday, our closest friends gathered on the few bits of furniture still left in our home, drinking wine out of plastic glasses, so unlike any of the celebrations we'd hosted in the past 16 years. That was probably the only time we ever got together without laughter.

After we said our goodbyes that evening and our friends left, John gave me an early birthday present. It was a beautiful gold ring with a gold nugget in the center to remember Rossland, the little gold mining town that we grew up in as a married couple and a young family.

As we left our friends, our church and our home behind, I knew something precious had ended. I knew change was in the future, but of course I had no idea how drastic the changes would be.

Chapter 13

Early on my 37th birthday we loaded the last of our things into the moving truck and loaded our own van with children, my mother (who was helping us move), two cats, personal blankies and stuffed animals, and left Rossland for the 400 km trip to our new home.

We had chosen to buy one of the houses that we looked at during our weekend from hell, and while it wasn't my idea of a beautiful home, it was quite perfect for us. Each of the kids would have their own bedroom, there was plenty of room for us to entertain, and it had a nice view. The neighbourhood had other young families in it, and it seemed like a good place to continue raising our family.

The day after we arrived in Enderby we went to church and felt the familiar feeling of being surrounded by God's family. We saw some familiar faces and were immediately introduced to others. We were very warmly welcomed and it confirmed to us that we were exactly where we were supposed to be.

Even though there was a Christian school in the area, we really were not in any position financially to send our kids, so we continued home-schooling. I say that like it was the easiest thing on earth to do, but really it wasn't. There were a few home-schooling families around, but nowhere near the support system we had in the Kootenays. It was a bit lonely for us all at times. Yet God knew what He was doing; home-schooling would provide us with a safe haven in the years to come.

Fully expecting the restlessness John had been experiencing to get better for him now that he'd taken on a new job, I was disappointed when only eight months after our move he became even more troubled than before. I couldn't put a finger on what was bugging him. He didn't share anything with me as he would have in the past, and slowly he began to pull away from me. We began fighting over little issues.

I blamed myself. I believed that if I was skinnier, prettier, sexier, more compassionate or empathetic, he would love me more. Our relationship was beginning to change from being best friends to being just an odd married couple.

I didn't want to be odd. I didn't want to be just married. I wanted my husband to continue being my best friend.

June 9, 1998 journal entry: *Things are gently falling apart and I feel quite helpless to stop them. I know I can't change anybody, only myself. Again I feel so helpless to change. Where do I start? I keep asking God to change me.*

There is something about the feeling of losing a friendship that hurts more deeply than anything else; even more so when you can't see or understand the reasons for losing it. It doesn't take long for that loss to cut deep into your soul.

June 16, 1998 journal entry: *On the inside, I feel like I am waking up every morning with less and less of a reason to.*

Ten days after that entry I felt I had all the answers. I thought I finally knew what had been bothering John, and I was given new hope. Even though the circumstances were deceitful and negative, I was hopeful.

June 26, 1998 journal entry: *On Wednesday night John wanted to take me out...we went for a walk...we came to a bench and he told me to sit down...handed me a paper...told me he'd borrowed thousands of dollars and didn't tell me. That lie, he said, led to another and another and another until he was beside*

*himself. It explained his anger, depression, indifference and
financial worries...We've talked and talked...God has brought all
the pieces together at this time and convicted both of us in
different areas so that we were prepared to go forward
emotionally, spiritually, physically, and financially.*

The paper he gave me that night was a letter that he began
with "My darling wife." In that letter were the details of what
he'd done, but my hope came from the words he used at the end
of the letter. "I will never again be worthy of your trust – I will
have to live with that. I have to face what I've done to you, to our
marriage, to our future. I have been the cause of so much discord
over the last year – anger, impatience, lack of spiritual leadership
– the list goes on – all because I wasn't man enough to face the
issue. I'm not sure if I can ever make it up to you or the kids. I
love you so much...I beg for your forgiveness."

The money was a big deal, I suppose, but the worst part was
that I just could not understand how John could have lied to me
all that time. Yet the man who sat across from me that night was
one so sorry and seemingly so willing to make things work, I
thought things could only get better from there on in. How could
they not, when we both so badly wanted a stronger relationship?

Yet things didn't really get better. There was much more
going on that I just couldn't understand.

August 7, 1998 journal entry: *We're at it again. I shut down,
and am having a real tough time picking it all up again. I don't
have much desire to pick it up and keep trying...I am so tired.*

I suspected there was something more going on than just the
borrowed money, but had no way of knowing what.

Chapter 14

It happens to us all if we live long enough. We get cranky and we turn forty. Or turn forty and get cranky (toe-may-toe, toe-mah-toe). Okay, there might be people out there that don't get cranky, but I know for sure that forty happens; all of my sisters, several of my friends, and my husband all did. I knew it would be just a matter of time before I succumbed as well.

The realization that I, too, was pushing 40 hit me 13 months before the actual date. The year I turned 39 I realized I needed to make some changes in my life. It was that same year that I noticed a complete change in John. He went from being restless to downright cranky (coincidence that he had turned 40 within the previous year?) He appeared to turn cranky overnight.

It happened in Alberta on the night that my nephew got married. More accurately, it was that night when I vividly noticed a change in him. We had just come back to our hotel room from the wedding reception and tucked the kids into bed. I think I might have been cranky first because I said something to John that I knew would generate a response out of him. For the first time in our 17 years of marriage he ignored me (I don't know, maybe it was simply time). He completely ignored me as if he could not be bothered with me.

I became afraid. There was no specific reason to be afraid, but I wondered what was going on, knowing that something important had happened; something different than what he'd already been dealing with. Something more than borrowing money without telling me, and something more than lying to me.

Because he had turned 40 the year before I considered this to be the beginning of John's "crisis" for lack of a better word. I knew nothing about midlife crisis at that point, except that some men started wearing heavy gold necklaces, drove sports cars, and found young women to date when they became "middle-aged."

I gave the beginning of 1999 a title in my journal, "Diary of a Midlife Crisis." I started it shortly after we got home from the wedding in Alberta.

January 10-15 journal entry: *John is in Vancouver. I am taking this time to do a lot of thinking about us, me, him, our family. I am working through "Avoiding the Performance Trap" [book] which deals with healing grace.*

January 15: *John came home tonight...he's not interested in sex??*

January 22: *I am allowing John to feel whatever he needs to, and I am sure that any day now he will want me again.*

January 23: *Oh-oh. This morning I am convinced John is having an affair...many tears in private. By nighttime I am quiet, morose, and not sure of our marriage. John is grumpy and snarly. He stays up, out of our bed, half the night reading.*

January 25: *For fun I look up men's midlife crisis on the internet. Guess what? John is a typical man going through a midlife crisis. All the signs are there: no interest in sex, pulling away from spouse, worried about money, thinking about lost career chances, watching his daughter hit puberty. Now I understand...We go out for coffee and clear the air. We laugh a little.*

January 26: *I started working out today...*

That was the first month of 1999. The year that began with a defining moment when I noticed a dramatic change in John continued to be discouraging. There are no more journal entries for that year. In fact, for 20 months I didn't write a thing down.

While watching my husband go through changes that did not include me or allow me to help in any way, our little church family was also going through serious changes. Differences between people became fences, and eventually became walls that nobody seemed able to tear down or climb over.

There was a specific night when it seemed like both my floundering marriage and my struggling church hit me at the same time. John had gone to Quebec on a five-day business related event at the same time that our church elders had called a meeting to try to break down some walls. Because we knew of the meeting ahead of time, we composed a letter together, and on the night of the meeting I read it to the people that had gathered. It was our effort to try to help, to give support to the board of elders.

I came home from that meeting sad and somewhat angry that things didn't look like they would be repaired in our fellowship, and I really needed to talk to John. I called him at his hotel, knowing it was hours later in Quebec, but also knowing that he'd be waiting for my call (whenever he was away from home, we spoke on the phone every night to touch base with each other). That night, however, he wasn't in his room when I called that first time or any time in the next three hours. I became extremely concerned that something had happened to him, and I couldn't sleep. I kept calling, and finally at midnight he picked up the phone. It was 3 a.m. in Quebec. He told me he'd been walking all night.

I believed him on the outside, not having any concrete reason not to, but I think there were some seeds of doubt planted subconsciously that night. We never talked about it, but as the months and years went by I would often find myself wondering if he had actually been walking all night.

Our church wasn't able to work through the problems, and a great number of us felt we couldn't stay in the aftermath of what had happened. In our hopes for reconciliation we began meeting together, and as time went on and no reconciliation seemed apparent, we formed our own church family, calling it Faith Community Church.

Things were not getting better in our marriage; we fought a lot. Most often it was about nothing, yet it was always about the distance I felt between us. I wanted my old husband back. I wanted him to look at me like he used to – his best friend, his confidante, his love.

But he didn't. Whether he couldn't or he wouldn't, I don't know, but he definitely didn't.

Very slowly I watched him drift further and further away from me, and it was with the realization that I was losing my husband to something or someone that I turned 39. I decided to make some changes in my life before I turned 40, hoping that those changes would help me become a better person and help me keep my husband. If it was another woman he was drifting towards, I was going to put the one he had back in the competition.

I know, it's an age old attempt at a solution to an age old problem. (That and having a baby, and that was so not happening!) It rarely works, but I really believed for me it would be different.

I decided to start running. The only reason I chose running was because our friends and neighbors in Rossland, Mandy and Fulvio, had been serious runners. At the time I thought they were certifiably nuts to want to run, but now it seemed like a good idea. I found a book in the library that was specifically to train women with no running experience to be able to run 5 km.

I planned to get in the best shape I possibly could. As fast as I could.

In the process of my reading and planning, John decided to join me in my new venture. That was fine with me because doing something together could only be a good thing. Perhaps it would even bring back the spark.

One day around this time John and the kids came home from the recycling depot all excited. Somebody had left a box of puppies right outside the depot and the kids wanted to bring one home. Very wisely they knew they should ask me first. But I didn't want a puppy; I had never in my life asked for a puppy. We lived on a postage stamp property in a subdivision that was rather particular about order and everyone knows that puppies know nothing about keeping order. I said no thank you (or maybe just no). I might even have said we couldn't afford a puppy and they seemed to understand, but the kids talked John into going back there "just to look."

I knew I had lost that battle when they took a cardboard box and a towel along with them.

Sure enough, they came back with a cute little black puppy. And a plan...we would pick up a paper route as a family to pay for dog expenses. That meant that three times a week the six of us delivered papers at 6 a.m.

Oh, you remember my attitude towards mornings? Well, it was one thing to get up at that time to curl up in a chair and spend time reading or praying. It is quite another to add to that five other people, a dog, exercise, and having to get dressed. The dog wasn't the only one growling about the new routine. Add that to the fact that I felt my marriage was falling apart and you'll get the idea of my emotional state.

I really needed to start my running program (although I wouldn't know how much for many, many months), and so we decided that after we delivered the papers, the kids would continue on home while John and I went on our 30-minute training run.

Those first few attempts were torture. It was a program where you run for 30 seconds then walk for a couple minutes; over time you increased the running part and decreased the walking. Those first days of 30-second runs were torture. I watched the seconds pass, thinking I would leave a lung behind if I didn't get to stop soon. Yet I persevered and as time went on, we both discovered that we actually enjoyed the running, so decided to join our "certifiably nuts" friends for a half marathon the following year. That would be running for 21.1 km. Privately, it was my 40th birthday gift to myself.

I know, I'm not really that great at giving gifts, am I?

It wasn't until several months later that I realized that God was helping me put things into my life that would help me traverse the coming season of my life. He'd already called me to spend time with him each day (building my faith), drawn us all together (building my family), put good people in my life (building my friendships) and now he was pushing me into better physical shape (building my fitness).

He had one more piece to add to my life to prepare me in every possible way for the journey yet to come.

Chapter 15

The new millennium was fast approaching. While the masses worried that the world might end at the stroke of midnight, my only thought towards that was to buy extra macaroni and cheese. I had way more important things than the end of the world on my mind. My own corner of it was collapsing, so what difference would it make if the rest of the world went down as well?

Surprisingly, 1999 ended and 2000 began with the world going on the same as before while my own world, my marriage, was slowly coming apart. I felt helpless and seemed to have no options. As divorce was a word that I wouldn't even let my children use, it most definitely was not an option for me to pursue. So then what were my options, what was I to do?

These questions haunted me night and day.

John and I continued to do our running together, training for our half marathon in September of that year. It was getting easier, and I no longer felt like I would deposit a lung on the road as I ran.

I continued to spend time daily with God. I continued to spend time with my friends.

John began going to Vancouver quite regularly on business trips and more and more often we would be fighting. It didn't seem to matter what we started the fight about, it almost always ended with me begging for him to please tell me what was wrong, to please let me in. He would meet my requests with stony silence. I knew my husband was going through hell, but I had no clue what it was or how I could help. Consequently we were both in torment.

Beside my bed was the place where I regularly tried to regroup and gather some semblance of normalcy around me. It was far enough away from my children so they hopefully wouldn't hear my sobs, and if they poked their head into my room they wouldn't see me right away.

There came a day when I found myself in another puddle of snot beside my bed, and I knew that I couldn't continue living that way. I was a mess emotionally, and until John would allow me back into his life I couldn't appear to find a way to cope on my own.

With shaking hands and a pounding heart, I took the phone and phone book into the bedroom. I looked up the number of the Alliance Church in a city 30 km away where I knew one of the pastors and trusted that the staff there would know of a good counselor that could help me. Hesitantly I asked the woman who answered the phone if they had any names of Christian counselors, all the while feeling that this must be as low as a person could possibly get. I was admitting to needing help and it made me feel like a failure. I don't think I knew anybody who had ever needed counseling up to that point; it seemed like everyone could handle their own problems except me.

I was given Betty's name and phone number. She was a counselor who came to Enderby once or twice a week and, before I lost my courage, and still shaking all over, I called her. When I spoke to her, I tried to remain calm, not wanting to appear to need as much help as your average unstable person. Betty was incredibly kind and gentle as she asked me questions, trying to determine whether or not we needed a one-time visit or weekly ones, and then we set up an appointment to meet.

Only John knew that I was seeing a counselor. I was mortified that I needed help at that time. I thought that being a Christian meant that God would fix everything and only loser Christians needed counseling.

Apparently I was a loser Christian because Betty and I began meeting on a weekly basis. She listened to me as I poured out my heart, and without passing any judgment on me she helped me understand that I couldn't change anything about anyone else, only myself; and that I wasn't a loser at all.

As the weeks went by, we began to talk about what John might be going through and how I could best help him. In her opinion the best way to do that was to back off, to give John his space, and stop making demands on him. (Who, me?)

In my mind there plays a movie of one particular time in Betty's office. It was quite a small office, and she had it very dimly lit. She often did other things while talking to me, which made it seem more like a visit and less like a "session." This particular day she was sitting in her chair, leaning sideways, away from me, opening an envelope while talking to me. As she put the envelope down she said, so casually, "Well, whatever John's going through will be workable, Gerty. It's not so bad. I just had a woman whose husband told her he was gay. Now that would be something to work through."

I don't know why that scenario is frozen in my mind, but it's as clear as if it happened yesterday. Perhaps a scenario like that was to me the worst that could happen to anyone, I don't know.

Betty reassured me that I would get through this. She prayed with me at every visit and I didn't feel quite so alone and hopeless.

From the outside looking in we were a family that had a lot going for them. John had a great job; I was able to stay at home with the kids; we home-schooled; we were active in our church;

we were involved in the community. As far as I knew, no one suspected there was anything wrong. Even if someone had asked, I wouldn't have known how to tell anyone what was happening. I hid the guilt and shame of not being able to keep my marriage together.

One Sunday afternoon in May of that first year of the new century, we took our youth group to hike the Enderby Cliffs. It's a fairly rigorous mountain hike, taking a couple hours to go up the 4,100 feet. While we were coming down five of us got separated from the rest of the group and found ourselves lost. We knew we had wandered off the correct path when we suddenly found ourselves forging through brush and branches and couldn't see a defined path. Common sense said we should have just sat down at that point and waited for help, but it was decided instead to continue to move. It was thought that as long as we headed downward we'd eventually get to the bottom.

It didn't happen quite like we planned, and we found ourselves rather hopelessly lost on a mountain in bear and cougar territory, two adults and three teenagers, one of whom was asthmatic and had left her medication in a friend's backpack. The only food between us was half a salami.

As the hours went by and we seemed no closer to finding our way through the bush, I thought about my life with John (naturally, as our problems never, ever left my mind). Part of me was hoping that we would be stranded on the mountain overnight so that John might think he could lose me and realize how much he really loved me. As much as I was terrified to stay on that mountain overnight, with all the potential for disaster, I so badly wanted this to be a turning point for our marriage. Kind of a shock therapy for John.

Another part of me was getting more and more worried about spending a night on a mountain with wild animals in temperatures that could still drop quite low.

Three hours after the rest of the group made it down, we managed to get to the bottom, quite a distance from where we should have been. We walked out just as Search and Rescue was preparing to go up to find us. When John spotted me coming down the road, he ran up to me and hugged me so tight; he seemed so relieved that I was okay. My heart thrilled with hope that he'd had enough of a shock and this would be the turning point in our marriage. He must have come to his senses, I figured, once he came so close to losing me.

If he did, his senses certainly didn't last long. His demons were still there, and before we knew it we were back on our rollercoaster of hell.

While I was desperately, and secretly, trying to hang on to our marriage, our dear friend Rick Zufelt was desperately trying to hang on to life back in Rossland. At 35 years old, he was fighting a battle with cancer and not winning. It was so difficult to be apart from all our friends there at the time.

On June 29, 2000 Rick lost that battle and went to spend eternity with the love of his life, Jesus, leaving behind his 24-year-old widow, Tiffany. Rick (and Tiffany's) friendship meant so much to John and I over the years, and it was painful to have to say goodbye. Just as five years previously John had a role in Rick's wedding, he now had one in his funeral as a pallbearer. At the end of the service, after the singing of Have Thine Own Way, the pastor asked who would carry on the torch for Rick. I watched as John, without hesitation, stood up to signify that he, along with the others that were standing up, would carry the flame for Christ that Rick carried in his life.

As I also stood, I felt another flicker of hope. If John was promising to carry Rick's torch, there had to be hope. All of this must just be a phase that we'd get through. While I waited for the getting-through-it stage to come, I took my torment to God, to the place that he prepared me for so many years earlier, those quiet hours early in the morning. I still hated getting up early and I still had a hard time disciplining myself to concentrate on my readings and my prayers, but I had come to treasure having that peaceful time alone with Him. As the year progressed and my agony grew, my prayers were often reduced to a simple, "Oh, God." There was often nothing else I could say.

"Oh, God" was enough for him to hear.

It was during one of those quiet mornings in September 2000 with my "prayer blanket" covering me that I read some verses that I began to cling to.

> *"But now, this is what the Lord says – he who created you, O Jacob, he who formed you, O Israel:*
>
> *'Fear not, for I have redeemed you; I have summoned you by name; you are mine.*
>
> *When you pass through the waters, I will be with you; and when you pass through the rivers, they will not sweep over you.*
>
> *When you walk through the fire, you will not be burned; the flames will not set you ablaze.*
>
> *For I am the Lord, your God, the Holy One of Israel, your Saviour.'"*
>
> *Isaiah 43: 1-3a*

It was at this time that our half marathon was scheduled, and we had prepared ourselves to the best of our ability. Part of our training was to run the 21.1 km a couple weeks before the actual race, and one beautiful Saturday morning we did just that.

We were well past the halfway mark, and it was getting warm. We were running on the highway which winds through some farming territory; I was running in front of John. I noticed ahead of me an irrigation system in full force, looking so cool and wet and refreshing that I moved over and planned my steps so that I'd get a light sprinkling. As I ran through the mist, I gave an exuberant "Woo-hoo!!" as the cool water hit my sweating body.

"Oh, John!" I hollered behind me, "That felt so good; you should run through it!"

There was no response until he got closer to me. "Uh, Gerty?" he asked.

"What?"

"Take a look back at that irrigation."

I swiveled around to see what he meant and noticed the different colour of the sprinkling stream; it wasn't water that was being spread on those fields...

The day before our half-marathon we traveled to Vancouver Island where Mandy and Fulvio now lived and the race was being held, taking a six hour drive and a two-hour ferry ride to get there. Naturally the kids came along with us; the older ones were going to watch the younger children, and together they were all going to cheer us on.

Afraid that I wouldn't sleep, I took a couple motion-sickness tablets before bed that night. I slept well, but the next morning I had a sleep-hangover (induced by those tablets). I also had severe cramps because it was the heaviest day of my period, and I felt like an emotional wreck.

Consequently, those were the longest and hardest 21.1 km I had ever run (okay, it was only the second time I had run that distance, but it was very, very difficult). The hills seemed like mountains, the flat stretches felt like hills, and the distance seemed to span the province. Yet I finished, and I experienced a sense of accomplishment like I had never experienced before. It was the best birthday present I had ever given to myself.

I was in the best shape of my life when my 40th birthday rolled around in October, yet it had been a long time since my husband had turned to me to make love. In an unfortunate twist of events, I can remember with clarity the night that we last made love (the date, what I was wearing, etc). Why? I don't know. How would I know that would be the last time? I didn't, but I remember it clearly.

Turning 40 happened at the absolute worst time of my life. Yet again God knew what He was doing. I am the youngest of four girls and years earlier all of us sisters plus our mother and sister-in-law had started the tradition of celebrating a major birthday (40 and 50) by waking the birthday girl up and taking her out for breakfast as she was when she woke up; she was not allowed to shower, brush her teeth, comb her hair, or get dressed. After breakfast we would let her get gorgeous and spend the day shopping and then going out to dinner.

Now I was turning 40, and with everything going on there was not even a thought in my head of my sisters all coming from hundreds of kilometres away to help me celebrate. Yet not only did my sisters and mom carry on our silly tradition of being together whenever one of us hit the big 4-0, they came a day early so that they could wake me up on my birthday. We spent the day shopping, eating, and visiting. At a time when I so needed to know I was still loveable, there they were.

They had no clue what I was going through.

I also woke up on the morning of my 40th birthday to find out that my girlfriends from Faith Community Church had decided to celebrate with me by hanging up 40 bras and corsets all along the front of our house, along with a sign that stated something along the line of "Gerty's 40, honk in support!" I am still surprised that the neighbours didn't secretly put our house up for sale the next day.

The following Friday I made a gruesome discovery; I had contracted an STD. I was absolutely horrified because I know the only way I could have gotten it was from John. My mind began to reel with what this meant, and no matter which way I looked at it, I could only come up with one answer: John must be having an affair.

My world was rocked.

The next morning John handed me a note from Joanne which was the beginning of a scavenger hunt for my 40th birthday that she had set up. I was to pack an overnight bag and then follow the directions. It led me from place to place, stopping at one bistro for a hot chocolate, another restaurant for a donut, and then I was to spend some time by myself browsing in a bookstore (she knew how much I loved books and bookstores).

I followed all her directions, all the while still trying to wrap my brain around the fact that my husband had given me an STD. I didn't know anything about STD's; I really didn't want to know. Someone who has been faithful forever should not have to find information like that out.

When I arrived at the bookstore I was drawn to the health section. There I saw a book that would give me the information that I needed, but before I dared to take it off the shelf and look at it I wandered carefully through the whole store, making sure that Joanne wasn't lurking somewhere ready to jump out at me and yell "Surprise!" I certainly didn't want that to happen while I was holding a book about STD's.

Once I felt safe, I furtively took the book and with my back to the wall, giving me a view of much of the store, I began to find the information I needed. Information I could hardly register because my mind was so full of disgusting thoughts and images.

Eventually I learned what I thought I needed to know and took the last leg of my scavenger hunt, which led me to a hotel room in Kelowna (100 km from home) where Joanne and four other friends from the Kootenays were waiting to surprise me with a 40th birthday weekend celebration. That evening they dressed me up as an old woman, complete with knee socks and a cane, took me out for dinner, and then paraded me through The Grand Hotel and Casino.

It was a bittersweet weekend. While I was overwhelmed with the love that my friends showed me, I was in turmoil as to what my next step had to be with John. I wondered if I should confront him or even leave him? I knew I couldn't leave him; that would be cowardly. I wanted to make our marriage work.

All this was churning through my mind as I spent a weekend with dear, sweet friends, friends with whom I felt I couldn't in a million years share what I was going through, mostly because I didn't want them to think less of me or of John. Secrets, secrets, secrets.

After I came home from that weekend with the girls, I asked John to take a drive with me. I just couldn't keep it quiet. Part of it was that John was always the one that I would confide in, the one that I would go to when I needed to figure things out or when I needed advice. It was just natural that I confront him now. I parked the car and told him that I had an STD and then asked him flat out if he was having an affair. He vehemently denied having an affair but admitted to giving me the disease. He said he had had it as well, getting it from a swimming pool change room.

I believed him. He was my husband, my best friend! Yes, I was naïve. Hearing him deny it worked for me, thinking that I must have overreacted, and that there couldn't possibly be any other woman. I mean, what did I really know about STD's? (A few minutes of reading didn't give me near enough information.)

As it turned out, the STD wasn't severe and was easily treated and I went back to thinking this was all just a phase (perhaps believing this was the only way I could survive). I continued to try to fix my world.

October 23, 2000 journal entry: *Funny, isn't it, how you think things can simply not get any worse and then you wake up the next day and everything is worse? I was frustrated and angry and as a result I was emotionally spent. I tried to talk to John, but he didn't feel like talking. I ended up sobbing almost hysterically. There was no response from him at all. Nothing. Which scared me further. I asked him if he was at all interested in making this marriage work and his answer was, "I don't know."*

I got Sally Conway's book "Your Husband's Midlife Crisis" today and am looking forward to devouring it. John is in Vancouver again. Three days this time. Last week was four days. I get so scared when he goes there. Can I trust him? Will he find someone else? Has he found someone else? He doesn't seem to love me, need me, desire a marriage, or feel committed. He's given me no hope. And continues to give me no hope.

October 25: *Yesterday was a strong day. I spoke to Sarah and Deb about what their dad's going through. It breaks my heart...John called [from Vancouver] and we really had nothing to say. He asks me about my day. What can I say? I survive without you? I'm not any closer to finding a solution to our life? I'm learning to live without you? I'm coping as an empty woman without love? I don't think he'd respond well...I feel like he is doing his damnedest to hurt me.*

It is so difficult to pretend all the time. I have to put on this face for everybody at church, at youth group. Even for the kids. Oh, God, can you hear me?

October 26 journal entry:

Dear John,

Just when I think I could never be hurt more than I already am, the unbelievable happens and I get hurt deeper. I don't even know how to tell you how sorry I am that you are going through this. And how sorry I am that I am who I am and have contributed to this... You said today, "What I'm feeling has everything to do with you – lots of them positive and lots of them negative. I can't share them with you."

I don't know how to go on.

Why can't I, for once, be the wife you need? Strong, capable, loving, nurturing, caring. Why must I always cause divisiveness? Why do I always hurt you? Let you down? I'm so sorry for all the wrong I've done. What I wouldn't give to have been a completely different person, one that you could admire, respect, and love. Have you ever loved me?

I am releasing you, John. If you want out of this marriage, I give you your freedom. I can only pray that you will find someone more worthy of you.

November 7: *John and I talked. He figures I would be so much better off without him (and he most definitely was NOT meaning suicide). He says I would have more strength and resilience than I could imagine. He went on to say that he hates himself for what he is doing to me and has done to me, that he has "squashed" me.*

November 9: *I am living in a nightmare. A hell. It's like my husband has died and I need to mourn and grieve. Except that he keeps showing up again and no one else knows he's died. I have to live a double life.*

December 2: *We limp along, not speaking, not sharing, not together, and not touching. If I can't be allowed to help him during a difficult time, will I want to be with him when this is all over?*

December 6: *Last night it all hit me at once. I couldn't sleep and my mind wouldn't settle. There was such a feeling of hopelessness. Even if John gets through this, how do we begin to pick up the pieces of our shattered marriage? How do we begin to forgive? To trust? To love? To laugh?*

I began to cry in bed and John put his arm around me. How I miss his touch, his hugs.

December 8: *It's too big for me. I always thought that when faced with a huge challenge, I would rise to it. I guess not.*

God, this hurts, and I can't do it with who I am. Change me, change me, change me!

It was time to put up our Christmas tree again. Putting up the tree has always been a very important part of Christmas for us as a family, one of those traditions that developed over the years. Since moving to Enderby our tradition was to go to a tree farm together and pick out a tree. John and Connor would cut it down while we women would take pictures. Once it was home John would get it all ready in the stand and bring it into the living room where we'd have a place of honour all ready for it. Then John would string on the lights.

Once the lights were on, we would take out the ornaments that we had collected over the years; we would unwrap them, talking and laughing about them (so many were made by the kids when they were little) as we hung them up together.

When the tree was completely decorated, we'd turn on its lights and turn off all the house lights. Then we'd all hop in the car and drive up the hill where we could see into our living room and we'd admire our tree from outside.

Once back home we toasted our tree with eggnog and officially started the Christmas season with an appetizer party. For all of us it was the night that we felt started Christmas, and it wasn't done unless everybody could be there.

It was December 11, 2000, the day we chose to begin the Christmas season. The mood was not so festive, but keeping things appearing normal was becoming somewhat of a gifting for me, so we proceeded to do the tree thing. As usual, John put up the tree and put on the lights.

When normally we would begin to unwrap the ornaments and bring up past memories together, this year John just sat on the couch. The kids begged him to help but he wouldn't. Instead, he fell asleep. We all felt hurt and the kids and I quietly decorated the tree without him. It was quite obvious that he was removing himself from the family.

There was no drive to see the tree that year.

Once the kids went to bed I asked John if I could talk to him. I had had enough and I was close to my breaking point (although it seemed like that point just kept moving further and further down). I knew I couldn't go on like this much longer.

We sat down together and I took off my wedding ring.

With tears in my eyes, I turned to him. "I'm giving you your freedom, John. It's all up to you now. I ask that you give the ring back to me only when you are willing to make a commitment to me for the rest of your life, accept me as your equal, and share yourself with me."

I was not sure that I would ever see it again as I handed it over to him.

He was upset, but I'm not sure if it was because I was giving him an ultimatum and he wasn't ready to make a decision, or if he was saddened by the way things were turning out.

After a few moments, he quietly said, "I'll make you one promise. I don't know when, but when I'm ready to talk, I will."

December 18, 2000 journal entry: *Oh, God, why can't I change? God, can't you stop this pain? Oh, God, I just want to scream and scream and scream and scream and never stop. I don't understand anything anymore. Are you allowing Satan to destroy us? Why won't you step in to fix it? When will you stop allowing this to happen? Even though I ask you over and over to change me, you stand there silent and cold. You let my marriage fail and right now I hate you for that. You have everything at your fingertips and within your control, yet you do nothing.*

December 22: *I told John I was taking the kids to Chilliwack for Christmas. He asked me not to because he doesn't want to be alone. He said he was so far down he has to look up to see the bottom. He actually said he was so sorry for what he was putting me through. I told him I would gladly go through it all if I could just go through it WITH him, beside him, helping him.*

At the end of it all, he did give me a long hug.

December 27: *I was hoping for a miracle on Christmas – some surprise or something from him. A hug or caring of some sort. Nothing.*

And so the first year of the new millennium ended. It was the worst year I had ever experienced.

Chapter 16

January 2001.

Every new year brings with it the feeling of promise and hope, a chance to get things right, to do something better.

For us it all just rolled from one day into another. Shortly into the new year John went to Vancouver for a few days to think things through. While he was away, I went to a movie with two girlfriends, Ingrid and Joan. I was sitting between them, munching on popcorn when one of them asked me a question. I don't remember what the question was, but I remember popping a piece of popcorn into my mouth before I gave my answer, as casually as I could.

"Well, right now my husband is in Vancouver trying to decide whether or not he wants to be married to me."

I popped some more popcorn into my mouth while I realized what I had just said and they processed what I had just said.

I'm not sure who was more shocked at those words, them or me. Joan and Ingrid knew nothing about what had been going on in my marriage, and this was the first time I had dared to voice anything about our problems to anyone besides Betty. It wasn't something I had planned to tell and certainly not something they expected to hear. I wonder if I had just reached the end (I wondered how many "ends" were there that I could come to?) and God decided to take over. I wondered if God knew it was time to share it? He would prove to be right (surprise, surprise).

After the movie, the three of us sat in the car and I shared the turmoil John was going through and how, consequently, my life had blown up. I told them that I thought maybe he was having an affair and that I was no longer wearing my wedding ring. I cried, they cried. It felt so good to have shared with someone. I felt a little less lonely in my pain. They promised to pray and I knew without a doubt they assaulted heaven for me.

A couple days later John came back home. It was a Monday evening. January 8. It became one of those dates that draws a line in your life where suddenly there is a before and there is an after.

The kids and I were playing a game at the kitchen table. There was nothing of the old times when dad's homecoming caused a huge fanfare. Everyone was a little more cautious, a little more nervous, and so we just kept playing. I made a huge deal of having fun without him, trying to show him what he was missing (so many last ditch efforts in hope one would just snap him out of this phase).

John puttered around the house while we played, showing no interest in joining us. Once the kids were in bed he asked if he could talk to me in the bedroom. He hadn't wanted to talk to me for so long (I was always the instigator of any discussions) that I immediately felt hopeful. Hopeful that what was about to happen would be the beginning of something different and better for our family.

Still always hoping.

As I walked into our room I heard soft music, saw two wineglasses and a bottle of wine. To me this was a lifeline; obviously something good was about to happen. Everything pointed to a new beginning, a change, or a closure to an agonizing time; the promise of a renewed relationship. My heart began to melt.

There was a chair facing the bed and he sat down on it, leaving me to sit on the edge of the bed. He poured us each a glass of wine, then put the bottle aside, but we both ignored the glasses as he took my hands in his. I knew something was about to happen; there would be change. I had thought about a moment like this for such a long time; there were several scenarios that might unfold in the next few moments. I wasn't so naïve to think that he would simply declare his love for me and the world would be right; I fully expected to hear news that I wouldn't like, but I had also rehearsed it all, so I knew I was ready to forgive whatever he confessed to.

I was so prepared for him to admit to an affair, the most awful thing that I could imagine happening to our marriage. I knew instinctively that this was about to be the defining moment. I was about to cross over from the before to the after, and I had no doubt in my mind that we would enter that part together.

He looked so serious when he looked me in the eyes and said, "I have something to tell you and you'll have to be very strong."

You'll have to be very strong.

Strong was something I was prepared to be if it meant a new beginning. I was so sure there would be a new beginning after he told me whatever awful news he had been holding on to for so long. Inwardly I was bracing myself for the support role that he was asking me to take.

I was prepared to be the Proverbs 31 woman - the woman of noble character, capable, one who will greatly enrich her husband's life, not hindering him, but helping him all her life, strong, clothed with strength and dignity, laughing with no fear of the future, wise and kind. I was going to be that woman. I would crawl right into her skin that night and everything I said and did would be just like her.

I think I was prepared to understand almost anything at that point. Except for the two words he uttered next.

"I'm gay."

Just like that. Gay. (Just a side note – gay is so not covered in Proverbs 31.) Gay? Excuse me? Gay? Did my husband of almost 20 years, my best friend, the father of my children, just tell me he was gay? Seriously? Gay?!?!

While my mind was reeling from those two words, I vaguely heard the end of his sentence, "and I think I need to leave our marriage," but it didn't register just yet.

I was still stuck on the gay part. How could he be gay? It just didn't make sense. We had sex (at least we used to), we had four children. Maybe he just thought he was gay.

It's funny in a way where one's mind goes when it receives news that is just not believable. My thoughts went from the word "gay" to our children.

Our children! As I was trudging through the sludge that was now oozing into my mind, our four children were sleeping peacefully, probably falling asleep easily when they realized their mom and dad weren't fighting again. Perhaps their dreams were sweet, dreams of our family becoming whole again. They were 16, 15, 13 and 10 years old.

Then the second part of his sentence slowly registered. Leaving? No, that couldn't happen. I wanted my ring back, I wanted to stay married, and so I said the only thing that I thought was acceptable and right.

"I forgive you."

Like I said, I had prepared for this moment, and this was all I had prepared. "I forgive you." I honestly believed we could work around the gay issue, we could still make our marriage work. Surely it wasn't the end of the world.

The rest of the night was a blur to me. I remember ripping pages out of my journal and hanging over the toilet. I cannot remember if I was flushing the pages or throwing up. I cannot remember if I cried, and I don't remember going to bed that night.

I do know that I hung on to the fact that he did not say that he was for sure leaving our marriage. He said "I think." I hung on to that like a drowning person would a life ring, thinking that once he saw how hard I was willing to work to help him, he'd decide to stay with me.

I would fix this. With everything I was I would show him how wonderful I could be, and we would fix our family.

The next day we went out together and talked. We talked just like we used to, as best friends. During that conversation, however, he made it very clear that he wanted out of the marriage. There was nothing to discuss, he had made up his mind, having all the details in place already. He had obviously given this a great deal of thought and planning.

We were less than five months away from our 20th anniversary, and I realized that my husband was truly leaving me. For a man. I was so humiliated.

I came home and huddled in my familiar corner of our bedroom, the phone clutched in one hand. I dialed Ingrid's number and said the words out loud for the first time.

"He's leaving me."

And then I burst into tears. Ingrid immediately began to cry with me. Nothing needed to be said, even if I could; that someone was sharing it with me was enough. The very, very difficult part was that there was no way I could tell her the reason. From that moment I knew I wouldn't tell anyone that my husband was gay.

January 10, 2001 journal entry: *It's over. The proverbial fat lady has sung. He's leaving. I started ripping this journal up because it was supposed to have a happy ending. It's not. After 20 years John has been completely honest with me. He has lied for 20 years! Last night we spent hours talking. He still is my best friend; he just can't be my husband.*

Not even in my journal could I utter the words that John was gay or give any details that might give the real reason for him leaving.

Even though he made it abundantly clear that he wasn't staying in the marriage, I would not give up hope for the future with him. I was going to let him go (like I could have stopped him), but I would leave the door open for him to come home. One of the ways I was going to do that was to keep his homosexuality a complete secret. In my mind, when he wanted to come back, there would be less healing and hurt for him to deal with; we would keep his homosexuality a secret between us.

That seemed like a really good plan. At the time.

There was no doubt that God was working in my life. Even though this was not what I wanted, there was some relief in knowing what was going on. With a strange sense of comfort, there was now a plan, and while it was not one of my choosing, it was at least a direction to move. And God was always ahead of me. For six months previously he was preparing me. He allowed circumstances to happen so that I would work through anger, depression, grief, and denial. I spent those six months crying, sobbing, screaming, nagging, whining, and pleading.

Now in the midst of it all I felt a strange calm.

The first week after John told me was a good week. I know that sounds so bizarre, but it was good. For the first time in over a year we were talking again, sharing, listening, and caring. We spent hours together alone, enjoying what we had always been to each other, best friends.

I finally knew the whole story, and there was such a sense of closure with that knowledge. We talked about the future, and we talked about the immediate. Sporadically I tried to tell him how we could work this through together and that I still loved him, but for some reason that didn't seem to be so important then. I think I was just so relieved that I had my best friend back that I almost didn't care about the future; right then I was in the most comfortable, beautiful place in the world: with him physically and emotionally.

We decided that it would be best if he didn't leave for a few weeks. I felt like I really needed to have all my "duckies in a row" before we told the kids so that I could be there for them and give them all they needed. I was going to have to learn everything about our finances, which meant learning how to pay the hydro, phone and gas bills; how to make mortgage payments and how to keep our insurance going. Not to mention all the ordinary stuff like mowing the lawn, changing a light bulb, knowing where the fuse box was, how to check the oil, and fill the window washer fluid in the car. Everything that John had taken care of for almost 20 years I would now have to learn.

John was more than willing to help me with whatever I needed, and that first week was the most peaceful we had had in a very long time.

The downside of us being best friends again was that John slipped in to the best friend mode and shared with me all the details of his journey. He told me of his first time in a gay bar and leaving again, the different men he had met, the fun he had with them. He shared with me who he was leaving me for. At the time it seemed okay to be hearing all that, but it most definitely came back to haunt and hurt me when the reality of our lives set in.

Nine days after his announcement, the reality of my life hit me. I was lying in bed reading a book and in there was the description of a man spooning behind his pregnant wife in bed, caressing her tummy. It brought back the memories of being pregnant all four times, how much I loved being pregnant and feeling my body change, and then the memory of Connor's birth: John standing behind me, so excited, yelling, "It's a boy! It's a boy! It's a boy!!!" That memory started a flood of baby memories and of things past. I cried and cried and cried.

That same night Sarah woke up with one of her night terrors, screaming that there was someone outside her window (she did this quite regularly, but I could never get used to being wakened by a blood-curdling scream from my own child). By then I was completely unable to sleep and all the questions raced through my mind. What if John so messes up his life that he loses his job? What if he gets tired of supporting us? How will I deal with the kids alone? What will it be like night after night after night alone in bed?

January 26, 2001 journal entry: *Today I feel rejected. John is so excited about it all. He tries not to be, but I can see it in everything he does. He's got an apartment rented and has a trip to Vancouver planned to pick out furniture. I'm feeling discarded and don't think he'll even wait to move out. I suspect that after we tell the kids next weekend and he goes to Vancouver, he will want to go at least a week earlier...*

...It's starting to hurt again. I'm starting to believe again that I'm flawed, not worthy, rejected, and unlovable. I'll never be held again to be comforted, to be desired, to be sought after. I'll be branded single, separated, divorced. I won't be able to take pride in the years we've spent together or cherish the memories we've made. Nobody to giggle with in bed, no one to choose things for my stocking at Christmas. No one will look up to me – they'll all pity me...

...I was hoping this pain wasn't going to come back and hurt like this again. I want to be married to John. I want us to be happy together and have a long future. And he just wants out. He figures he'll be happier without me. You know, I haven't seen him shed a tear over this at all. There seems to be only excitement.

I'm crying too hard to continue.

The next day I went into Kelowna, looking for any Christian books on homosexuality or anything that might help me. I was disappointed when I couldn't find any, but I think God had another reason for me to be in Kelowna that day. I had been contemplating the empty finger on my left hand that had for over 20 years worn a ring signifying that I belonged to someone. I didn't like the idea of an empty finger, and was considering getting myself a ring that represents my commitment to God, belonging to him and his supporting me.

I walked past a jewellery store and on impulse went in, which was unusual for me. Something in the display case grabbed my attention: a gold ring with a cross of diamonds. It happened to be half price and seemed absolutely perfect for what I had been contemplating, and so I bought it. (Five months later I went back to that same jewellery store and they noticed my ring. When I told them that I had bought it there earlier that year, they said they had never seen a ring like that before, was I sure I had bought it there?...I like to think it was God's idea.)

That day I wrote in my journal, *I will wear this ring where my wedding ring was to symbolize that God is my "husband." A reminder that He will be forever faithful and that I need to be faithful to Him; that He will be my provider, my lover, my encourager, my support, my strength, my tower, my reason to live. I will put it on the day John moves out.*

*"For your Maker is your
husband –
the Lord Almighty is his name –
the Holy One of Israel is your
Redeemer;
He is called the God of all the
earth."
Isaiah 54:5*

Three weeks after the announcement and four days before we planned to tell the kids, John and I met with the elders of our church. John explained to them that he had been going through a difficult time for the last few years. He told them that he needed time and space and therefore he had decided to leave his marriage. At first the men were quiet, but expressed support. As the minutes went by, however, they became bolder in what they said to John. At the end of an hour they were all weeping, praying, and pleading with John not to do this. One of our elders turned to John with tears running down his face. "I've noticed for some time you've been burdened. I don't know what it is, but whatever you are seeking, John, is it worth the price you are paying? When an intruder comes into your home, you would do whatever it took to protect your children. You would give your very life to protect them from harm. John, something far worse is about to enter your home and destroy your children."

What struck me was John's reaction to this all. He sat there almost emotionless. I am sure some of those words hurt but with all of us crying, he remained unmoved. And that scared me. Was his heart completely hardened? Was he no longer able to distinguish right from wrong?

The elders told us that they were going to pray for a miracle and I told them they had four days before we told the kids. When they asked John if he was willing for a miracle to happen, he answered, "I don't know."

The next day the board fasted and prayed for us.

Journal entry that day: *I am overwhelmed by the moral response of these men. There is such strength in knowing they will support me and the kids and always be willing to accept John back with open arms.*

The next four days dragged by. The miracle never happened and we planned to tell our children news that would destroy their hearts.

Chapter 17

Slowly the time came for things to get worse. Up until now very few people knew what was happening in our marriage. And no one knew that John was gay. If it were up to me, no one would find out, not even my best friend, Joanne.

The weekend to tell the kids and then our church family arrived. It was a Saturday afternoon when we sat our four children down in the living room. They knew something was up because the only time we called them all together was for big news (usually the Disneyland-type news). We told them that things weren't going so well between us and that we were separating for a while. Deborah was the first to cry.

Caitlin was 13 years old at the time and for the last eight months had been wearing a daughter ring on her left hand. John and I had bought each of our daughters a gold ring when they turned 13; a ring with three stones - the center one was her birthstone and the two on either side of it were John's and my birthstones. As Caitlin heard the news that we were separating, she took off her ring and threw it on the floor (to this day she has not put it on again), bursting into tears.

Connor listened and watched and then also began to cry. Sarah was the only one who remained stoic and strong for a bit before saying that it was actually a relief because she'd been expecting it for a long time. Those words hurt because I realized all the things I'd tried to hide from them that I never actually did. They'd heard so much of our fighting, my crying. Hearing my child say it's a relief that her mom and dad were separating was like a knife in my heart.

At one point Deborah voiced the thought that this was all wrong. Eventually nobody had anything else to say and we all went our own ways. Later on, to try to help our kids know that we were still a family, and to give them a venue to talk it out, we decided to take them out for dinner. In the darkness of the car on the way to the restaurant some of their feelings came out.

"You're running, dad," said Sarah, from the back seat. "You never really tried and both of you are the reason that I never want to get married."

Ouch. How I wished I could have said that she didn't understand; that, in fact, her dad was gay, and it wasn't my fault! But I couldn't, so instead I added another pain to my heart.

Deborah's voice came next, "The reason I haven't been kissing you goodnight lately, dad, is because you make mom cry." Another ouch. Then Caitlin also started to cry.

Taking four broken and hurting children to a restaurant when their world was falling down around their ears was not the most brilliant idea we had ever had. There was no conversation, nothing to really say; they needed time, not togetherness.

At bedtime Connor lay in bed and cried in John's arms and then mine for almost an hour. We tried to comfort him, but it didn't seem to ease his fears. Eventually Connor crawled into bed with us, and his little 10-year-old voice said, "I'm going to miss dad...do you have to do this?...how long is dad going to be gone?...will we still get our allowance?...where will we get money?" We answered all his questions and tried to reassure him, but he just sobbed and sobbed.

I couldn't understand how a father could do this to his child. The knife in my heart just kept twisting and it was John that was holding the knife. He had the ability to remove the blade, but chose to keep it in. I could not understand how he could not break down in tears and ask us all for forgiveness; how he could want gay sex more than these precious children; how he could just watch the relationships he'd built for almost 17 years slowly die and not step up to repair them.

The following day was Sunday and we stayed home from church. One of the elders had asked me the day before if it would make it easier for me if he announced our separation to the church, rather than me having to make the announcement. I was more than willing and very grateful to him for that. None of us were at that service, but I heard afterwards that the announcement had been met with shock and tears.

February 6, 2001 journal entry: *...so many people have called and come over. It is overwhelming. One of my challenges is to accept what people offer. To be a friend and have friends.*

In the two weeks that followed before John physically left us there was an outpouring of love from our church family.

I kept a list of people and acts that touched our family in some way or another. There were 45 people on that list. You have to understand that our congregation didn't total 100 at that time, including all the kids.

Some people sent flowers, some gave helpful books. Most people sent us cards to let us know they were praying for us. One dear friend just showed up with a magazine and a chocolate bar. The Sunday before John moved out, while he was in Vancouver buying furniture (yup, that's how he spent the last weekend with his family), there was a knock on my door. I opened it to Yolanda, a friend from church that I didn't know all that well yet. She stretched out her hand to me and in it was a pint of Haagen Daaz chocolate ice cream. She gave me a hug and cried. No words were necessary.

After dinner that night I went into the living room and lit some candles. Then I brought out the ice cream and enough spoons for all of us. We sat around the living room table eating ice cream out of the carton. We made an occasion out of the friendship that was shown to us and used it to create a memory.

There was no doubt in any of our minds that we were loved. So many tears were shed on our behalf in that particular time. One friend, who lived in the Kootenays, told me that she saw me in one particular scripture passage and as much as I denied it, it gave me strength to keep on going. Ironically, it was part of Proverbs 31, that woman that came to mind on the night John told me he was gay.

> *"She is clothed with strength and dignity;*
> *she can laugh at the days to come.*
> *She speaks with wisdom,*
> *and faithful instruction is on her tongue.*
> *She watches over the affairs of her household*
> *and does not eat the bread of idleness.*
> *Her children arise and call her blessed;*
> *her husband also, and he praises her:*
> *'Many women do noble things,*
> *but you surpass them all.'"*
> *Proverbs 31:25-29*

And then came the day came when my husband of almost 20 years actually left me. The day he was able to walk out of our home, away from his best friend and wife, and away from his children.

February 17, 2001 journal entry: *D-day. Dad's departure day. It's actually happening. No amount of words and prayers have stopped it. I spent the last night ever with my husband's arms around me. I wonder if any man will hold me again...*

... I feel like this is an historic period. The end of a journal, the end of a journey, the end of a relationship as it was, the end of a family as it was, the end of a woman as she was. I think back four months ago and remember that I thought I could find an answer because I finally knew the question. How I tried to help John, tried to fix our marriage. And how God slowly picked me up to prepare me for when it all fell apart. And now John's moving out...

...I learned that God loves me more than I will ever understand and probably never fully accept....

...This is the end of almost 21 years together. We began as friends...now we separate...I will miss him more than I can express. I will ache without him, I will be incomplete without him, I will never be the same woman without him...

Goodbye, my best friend, my love, my heartbeat, my other half. Find peace, find happiness, and then find your way back home. I will wait.

Chapter 18

Sarah had just turned 17, Deborah was 15, Caitlin 13, and Connor 10 when John walked out of our lives.

When it was time for him to leave, on February 17, 2001, he hugged each of the kids except Sarah, who refused his embrace. I walked him to the door as if he were a guest I was saying goodbye to and he hugged me. Hugged me good and tight. I have to admit, it felt so good to have him hold me like that. It felt like he might still need me.

I had made plans for this night, trying to make this first night on our own one we got through together without a huge fuss. As such, the kids and I dragged all our mattresses and bedding into the living room and put them side by side, like a family bed. It was still early in the evening, but we closed all the curtains, put on our jammies, and settled in to watch a movie. Just before we started the movie, I found Connor in his room crying. As I was consoling him, I was so sad for him. I had lost a husband, but this little guy was losing his dad; I couldn't begin to understand the pain he must have been feeling.

After the movie, we all got ready to go to sleep. With the lights off and all snuggled in our beds, I asked the kids how they were doing.

If it wasn't so heart-wrenching, it might have been comical. One child would share a thought or feeling and then start crying, so I'd climb over the others to comfort her/him. Then another would start crying and I'd climb over the other way to comfort that one. I did a lot of crawling and we did a lot of crying together that night.

Aside from the oven timer going off at 2:38 a.m., we survived our first night alone.

Four days after John had left I was finally able to connect with my parents and so tell our family that our marriage was over, and that John had moved out. They had been out of the country, and as a result, none of my family knew what was going on (wanting my parents to know before the rest of my family, I chose to wait). My dad was shocked and speechless. The only words he seemed to be able to find were to ask me if there was another woman. I was able to assure him that there most definitely was no other woman in the picture. If he only knew...

I had a tough time with saying that over and over to people. To them, if there wasn't another woman, how on earth could John leave us? It just didn't make sense to any of them, and of course I couldn't really give any reasons. I simply told people it was something he just had to do.

The first two weeks alone were almost good weeks, where we all focused on ourselves and our blessings. My main purpose became being there for the kids. I believed that they still needed the feeling of family, even if it was nowhere near what it once was. They needed to know that one of their parents was completely there for them, that there was a constant in their lives. John came over at least once a week to have dinner with us. Some friends thought I was crazy for allowing him such easy access into the family like that, but at the time it seemed to be a good idea. He said he wasn't equipped to have the kids at his place at all and we both wanted the kids to see him as much as possible.

Yet I struggled more and more with watching him and his new life. He seemed to have everything he wanted, waltzing in and out of our lives when it suited him, telling us all about the fun he was having, the new recipes he was trying. We didn't do things well together, we still fought a lot. We both had different expectations and he had a new life.

After three weeks of being on our own, I decided that it was time for a special evening for the kids and me. I put a lace tablecloth on the table, set it with the best china, wineglasses, and candles. I made a cheese fondue followed by a dessert fondue. The idea was that we would relax together and I wanted the kids to know that we still mattered as a family. After dinner we watched a movie together and for a short time, we almost felt normal.

The following day the reality of being a single mom hit me hard when Sarah went on a "date." Although she insisted it wasn't a date, she went mini-golfing and out for dinner with a guy who really liked her. Sounded like a date to me.

Journal entry: *This [the first date] should be a time for me to share with a husband. We should be waiting up for her together, then snuggling in bed giggling over it all – young love. Instead, I have no one to share it with, no one to talk to.*

As the weeks went by I struggled more and more with John's homosexuality. Throughout my entire life I had known only three men who were gay, and I don't believe I even had a conversation with any one of them. It was so completely out of my world I really didn't know what to do with it. There weren't too many books out there that covered the topic of gay husbands. There were Christian websites that I found that were a help in my understanding of what John was going through, but I could only go to those when there was nobody around. And of course they were all about recovery and how to overcome homosexuality. It made me angry that John refused to think about the fact that he might not need to live his life out as a gay man.

There were so many things I could not wrap my brain around, like John knowing his whole life that he was gay. When he told me that I was the only woman he was ever attracted to and consequently was "his salvation," I didn't know what to do with that. When he told me that it was inevitable that he would "come out," I wondered how our marriage and I fit into that. I was tormented with what our marriage ever meant, if any of it was real, or if I was just a cover-up for John to look "normal."

I had no one to talk to. I was determined to keep this hideous secret. And it was slowly killing me, I think. All my journal entries have a vagueness to them because not even on those pages did I dare write that John was gay.

March 11, 2001 journal entry: *I always thought we had something special. Now I discover how tarnished it has always been. And I'm lost. I don't know my own point of reference any more.*

There are so many more blessings than hurts and I thank God for each one. But right now, all alone, it's the hurts that hug my heart, not the blessings.

I have to mourn the passing not only of my husband and lover, but also of my best friend. The only person I could really talk with, share ideas with, relate to 100 per cent. And to know now that I was never really that back to him is almost unbearable. The deepest thoughts and feelings he had that I now know he never could share with me. All the times I laid my heart open for him, thinking his was open for me, it wasn't. Which is why, now, he doesn't even miss me – he never really needed me or let me in so it wasn't that hard for him to just go away.

So much pain, hurt, anguish.

I alternated my agonies. I would agonize over how much of our marriage was actually a sham, if there was any honesty in the emotions John had for me at all. Then I'd flip over and wonder how much I was to blame. I couldn't help but think I had failed him. If I had been a better listener, would he have been able to trust me with his secret within our marriage? If I had been a more ardent lover would he have been able to be content sexually? How much of his needing to live openly as a gay man was my fault?

I didn't have any answers to those questions; I'm not actually sure there were any. But someone once said to me, much later, that no matter how lousy a wife I was, I never deserved John's unfaithfulness, his deceitfulness, or his leaving our marriage. Even though that didn't give me any direct answers, the message reached my heart and comforted me.

April 12, 2001 journal entry: *I don't want to erase 21 years of my life. I desperately want to hang on to those years and build on them. I don't know how to let go. What does God want? Does He want me to cut John out of my life or be there for him? How do I be friends with someone capable of such hurt and deceit? In an e-mail yesterday John said, "Yeah, I lied a lot and I'm not proud of it, but I would hope now that you could understand why I had to." If he so easily lied and deceived me as my most intimate friend, lover, and father of my children, why do I think he will be trustworthy now? Is he any better? Has he changed?*

As my friend, what would I expect from him? Honesty, caring, sharing...

...He cannot be my confidante, my best friend. Nor can I be his...Along with that thinking, I then need to build my trust in Jesus and let him be my confidante, my best friend, my listener.

As evidenced by that particular journal entry, I constantly struggled with where John fit in my life now that he was no longer my husband. I alternated with thinking we could still be friends and being angry at him within that quasi-friendship. Five days after that entry, I wrote him a letter.

Dear John,

Yesterday Sandra (a new friend of mine that was encouraging me with daily e-mails) mentioned that she heard that you were angry at God. I presume Sarah told her that based on a letter you gave her... I know the reason you are angry and I even understand that anger although only to a certain level because I've never been there.

But as I continue to work through our relationship, I continuously let my mind wander through all the good, the bad, the clear, the muddy. This morning I had this thought triggered by Sandra's comment: God created you, loves you, and knows you even better than you know yourself. He knew what your struggles would be even before you were conceived. He knew your personality, your strengths, and your weaknesses. What I believe is that when he gave me to you, and I was the only woman you ever loved and desired, it was for a purpose. It was to give you a life complete with love, children, happiness, companionship, a best friend. He knew you'd have to make choices, sometimes daily, but he gave you the support and framework to do that. He also knew that you would have to work harder than the average husband to keep our marriage intact, the passion alive. In a word, He knew how much you would have to sacrifice. But no more than he had to, to be able to give you the life you had. And as long as you remained true to him and me, things were okay.

Without a doubt, I believe that almost two and half years ago you made a choice to give up on our marriage. There were problems you couldn't face, issues you couldn't deal with, and you made a conscious decision to let everything good go and chose to give in to yourself. You turned 40 that year, and perhaps you realized that there was more out there for you to taste, and if you didn't taste it now you might never.

There were many things that I wasn't for you. If we had put our marriage first and worked on liking each other, respecting each other and putting the other first, could we have headed this off? I believe that with God's help we could have. We could have found resources. With much needed help I would have been able to deal with the truth and move on. I base that knowledge on my reaction of January 8 and until February 17, when you left.

The purpose of this letter is to maybe help you with your anger toward God and perhaps help you realize that none of this is God's fault or choice. That falls squarely on your shoulders and I think once you can accept that, you can understand God's role and accept it – full forgiveness and healing.

I don't write any of this to be husband and wife again. At this point I don't see that as a possibility. I'm not even sure that I can make that jump from wife to friend. I have a strong feeling that that is not my role in your life. My role was to be your wife, to share your life, and that is now over. A new season. And God's purpose for me with you is over.

Find healing, John, and reconciliation with the one who wants to hold your hand again and guide you through the rest of your life. The happiness you have found now is for only a short season. Come back to Him.

Chapter 19

Keeping John's homosexuality a secret was becoming a very, very difficult thing for me. Very naturally, friends wanted to talk about our marriage falling apart and how I was doing. While I needed to talk and was open to talking about it, the more I did, the worse I felt inside because talking about both those things meant I often had to pretend or even lie. I couldn't be honest about the cause of the breakup and without that, how I could I begin to explain how I was really doing? I could share so easily of what God was doing in my life, how He was meeting all our needs, minute by minute, but the pain in my heart, how I felt as a woman, I couldn't share with complete honesty.

Because of that, I would find myself at times ready to scream with no one to scream to except God. And while that is great, he doesn't have skin on, and sometimes I really needed someone who did.

I remember one of those days that things just unraveled from morning to night. I struggled all day with wondering why I couldn't just let John go, how I knew he was wrong in his actions and being quite selfish. I talked to him on the phone earlier that day and I realized that I just couldn't handle seeing him or talking to him. I just missed him too much. I hated myself for how I often treated him – like a nagging wife, always criticizing and questioning. I resented how much fun he was having and how much pain and work I was left with.

With all that going through my mind, I decided to take the dog out for a run. I knew I was near the edge, emotionally, so I was trying to ward off any serious outbursts.

Off I went down our usual country road. After a few minutes, the dog had to stop and take care of her business. When she was done I started off again, but was quickly stopped by the dog-poop-control people. I was handed a baggie and told to pick it up.

That was the ultimate worst-day happening, I tell you. To put my hand in a baggie and pick up poop from a dog I never wanted in the first place was more than I could handle. Yet I knew it was the only responsible thing to do because we weren't officially out of the city limits, so I asked if I could do it on the way back. You know, when it wasn't so, well, gross? She said no, I couldn't, and it all became just too much for me. I started crying and yelling at this poor innocent lady only trying to do her job, all while I was picking up dog poop.

It was nasty and scary for both of us, I'm sure. My journal entry that day read, *I keep replaying that scene in my mind and wonder if I'm losing my mind? How could I lose it like that? I'm really that mad at John, I think, but have no avenue to work that through. I just can't seem to get a handle on me with him. So much hurt, so much betrayal.*

As the days and weeks and months crawled by, I could see over and over again how God had orchestrated things to be in place. I kept up my running a few times a week; the physical exertion was one of the only places that I could get rid of the feelings I would have. I would often use to it to "chase my demons." When I got angry, overly sad, or just overwhelmed, running gave me back the perspective I needed. With each step that I pounded down, some of my negative emotion went with it; it was often the place where I poured it all out to God. By the time I finished a 5 – 10 km route, I felt I could handle things again. In the first few months after John left, I also ran once a week with a friend. We had visions of doing a half marathon in

Vancouver together. We ran at the same pace, were able to talk while running, and we began to share with each other. This friend was the first one that I admitted to that John had actually had an affair. I didn't specify the gender and I'm guessing she was thinking it was a woman, but I didn't care; it felt so good to just say that out loud. She prayed as we ran.

We never did run the half marathon. One day we began a 13 km training run and less than four km into it my body shut down. It simply refused to go another step and I realized that the stress in my life would not be relieved by overdoing it physically. I had to take a step back and ease up on pushing myself.

I was learning what worked for me and what didn't, as far as coping and overcoming was concerned.

When I had turned 40 and suspected that John was having an affair, I began what I call my drastic "gotta' get him back" strategy. I was already running and so I was in pretty good shape (for me, anyway), but I felt I could do more to win him back. And so I began taking care of me, pampering and appreciating myself as a woman. I took the time to care for my skin with nice creams, kept my legs smooth and generally made myself look as good as I possibly could.

Of course I had no idea at that time that I was competing against men. (I guess in some ways, it might be a good thing I lost...what would I have looked like if I won that competition?) When it became apparent that I wasn't going to get him back, I continued to take care of me because it turned out to be for me, not him. Again, God had it all place so that when I'd really need to know that I was woman enough, I did.

Once John left, I found that pampering myself was therapeutic. In some ways, it might be seen as selfish, but in the light of John's homosexuality it almost became essential that I felt feminine; that I confirmed within myself that it wasn't because of how I looked that drove John to embrace his homosexuality. Every Saturday night, almost without fail, I gave myself a pedicure and painted my toenails. It was healing for me.

As well as the physical pampering, I also allowed myself times of personal space. Because my weeks were so busy with the kids, home-schooling, and helping to run our youth group, I would give myself part of Saturday mornings to have my coffee in bed while reading a magazine. It was kind of a regrouping time and a time I cherished, uninterrupted.

In one of my introspective moments alone, I made up a list of reasons why life could be okay without John. It was my way of lightening up a heavy time and trying to see the positive.

1. I can get up when I want.
2. I no longer have to plan activities, days, and evenings around John.
3. When I choose to do something, it's because I want to, not because I have to.
4. Toilets are easier to clean.
5. The bathroom is now all mine.
6. There is very little ironing to do and who cares if I actually do it?
7. I can choose where all the money goes.
8. Everything is now my responsibility, therefore I take better care of everything.
9. Groceries cost less.
10. My personality is not influenced by what I think John wants me to be.
11. I have so many friends that I can now spend as much time as I like with.
12. I no longer rely on John to give me approval – I am learning that I'm pretty good just as I am.

13. I realize how much I have to offer, again, just as I am.
14. I can wash the sheets as seldom as I want.
15. I can eat in bed.

Chapter 20

We were learning to survive, to find a way live within the circumstances we found ourselves in.

One huge blessing in our lives, although quite in disguise (and sometimes in downright hiding!) was home-schooling. It gave all the kids a place to be real. If they had a tough night or were overwhelmed with it all, they could sleep later, stay in their pajamas, and not talk to any one. They weren't faced daily with having to put on a happy face or explain to anyone what had happened to their mom and dad. They had a place to sort through it all and we all understood. We plugged along with academics, but had more Pro-D days than school days. I suppose they were better called Mental Health Days. I believed that coming to terms with what life had become was infinitely more important than school work in those first months. It was a blessing for us all to be able to be together during such a horrid time.

There continued to be such an outpouring of love from people. God used so many friends in our slow journey to healing. Something very uplifting to me were the scriptures that friends would give me; scripture that could only be handed to them by God's prompting.

> *"For I am the Lord, your God,*
> *who takes hold of your right hand*
> *And says to you, Do not fear;*
> *I will help you."*
> *Isaiah 41:13*

"I will praise the Lord, who counsels me;
Even at night my heart instructs me.
I have set the Lord always before me.
Because he is at my right hand,
I will not be shaken.
Therefore my heart is glad and my tongue rejoices;
My body also will rest secure,
because you will not abandon me to the grave, Nor
will you let your Holy One see decay.
You have made known to me the path of life; you will
fill me with joy in your presence,
With eternal pleasures at your right hand."
Psalm 16:7-11

"Surely God is my salvation;
I will trust and not be afraid.
The Lord, the Lord, is my strength and my song; He
has become my salvation.
With joy you will draw water
from the wells of salvation."
Isaiah 12:2-3

Blessings were overflowing. I was afraid that we'd all begin to take them for granted and so I started a Blessings Book, a scrapbook with pictures of us covering the front of it. Everyone in the family was encouraged to write in. Whenever someone did something that "blessed" another person, it was written in there with the date and the action. Many times those writings were about people outside our family, and I was encouraged to see the kids writing those in there faithfully. As the weeks went by, they started noting down the things that their siblings or I had done. I would often find the kids looking in there to see if anyone had written something nice about them, and see them get excited when someone had. It was kind of a double blessing then and I saw how focusing on all the beautiful things and people in our lives really built us up.

John left in February. In April, Sarah, Deborah, and Caitlin all decided that they wanted to be baptized. This was a huge thing for them and for me. I found it to be quite an emotional time as I watched them prepare to publicly follow Christ.

The Sunday of their baptism began with us all having a special breakfast together. It was our family's tradition to begin special days, be it a birthday, Christmas or back to school, with a nice family breakfast and this day was no exception. As we sat at the table, I gave each of the girls a precious gift to remind them of the precious promises they were making that day in front of everyone.

In keeping with the theme of the ring that I now wore where my wedding ring used to be, I had bought each of the girls a piece of gold and diamond jewelry. The gold of the jewelry was to represent their lives – malleable and bright for Christ; the diamond represented their faith – invincible, strong, brilliant and fiery. Along with the gift, I gave them a poem I wrote specifically for that day about what their gifts represented and my desire for their lives.

Blessing of Gold and Diamonds

> *May your life shine as gold;*
> *Your faith last as diamonds.*
> *May your life radiate Christ;*
> *Your faith stand firm and strong.*
> *When the storms come*
> *To scratch and destroy,*

May your life be shaped and molded,
Your faith be your strength.
May your life always be God's gold;
Your faith God's brightest diamond.

That day our little church was decorated with balloons and streamers. It was a celebration of those being baptized, my girls and other teenagers that meant a lot to each of us there. Because we didn't own our own church building and as such we met in the community hall, the baptismal "tank" was not a nice built-in church model. In actuality it was some animal trough that the men of our church had borrowed. Fortunately it looked more like a hot tub than something for animals, so no one seemed to mind (and not one of my girls came out with, "Ew, Chilliwack!" so I guess it was well scrubbed).

John came to the service, which took immense courage on his part, and I have to say I was quite surprised. While no one knew that he was gay, they all knew that he had left us, and so I really didn't think he would show up. To see him there gave me great hope, thinking that if ever there was to be a change of heart, watching his three daughters be baptized would cause it.

John was welcomed by all our friends and then we sat together as we listened to each of our daughters share their testimonies. Sarah spoke of how she had always loved the song *Great is Thy Faithfulness*, and how when her dad left she had reached the lowest point in her life. It was there that God met her and His faithfulness became real to her, and she put all her trust in the one person who would never fail her. "I've probably done more crying in the last few months than I have in my whole life put together. Yet in the midst of my tears and struggling with more pain than I've ever known, he has taught me that, no matter what, he will always be there." She ended her testimony by sharing the bible verses that meant the most to her at that time.

"Because of the Lord's great love we are not consumed,
for his compassions never fail.
They are new every morning;
great is your faithfulness."
Lamentations 3:22-23

After she was baptized in the trough we all sang *Great is Thy Faithfulness* (just a few years later she would walk down the aisle to that same song on her wedding day).

Sitting beside John as Sarah poured out her heart and expressed the immense pain that her dad had caused her was difficult, but inside I was excited in a way. What sort of man could hear the hurt in his 17-year-old daughter's voice, knowing that he put that hurt there, and not be moved to change?

I didn't dare to even look at him; I would just allow God to do His part.

When it was Deborah's turn, she shared about giving her life to the Lord, and then she, too, focused on the most painful time of her life, her dad's leaving. She spoke of how, when her dad left, she had to depend on God totally. "When I'm in my room crying because of all that's going on around me, I can look to Him and know He's always there beside me. I love Him with all my heart and I'll try to serve Him in all that I do." Her favorite bible verse was found in the Psalms.

"My salvation and my honor depend on God;
he is my mighty rock, my refuge."
Psalm 62:7

Crying now, I just hurt for my girls. If I could have taken that pain from them and carried it myself, I would have. Right beside me sat the man that actually had that option. With just a word, he could be back in their lives and begin to ease the horrid anguish they were feeling as a result of his actions.

Again I couldn't even glance at him, I had to give him his total privacy with God.

By the time Caitlin came up to give her testimony, I don't think there were many dry eyes in the congregation. Caitlin, too, mentioned her dad leaving. "The biggest thing I've learned is that God loves me no matter what I've done, or who I am, no matter where I am. When my dad left, I felt my world crumbling. But I found support. I found support in my youth group, in my family and in my God...Jesus is the best friend I could ever have. He can not love me more and he will not love me less." The verse that gave her strength was found in Romans.

"And we know that in all things God works for the good of those who love him, who have been called according to his purpose."
Romans 8:28

It was heart-wrenching to hear Caitlin echo the sorrow and pain that her sisters had been feeling. Yet there was so much joy that morning knowing that in the worst scenario any child could imagine, they had all seen God's face and felt His love and were choosing to stay in His perfect peace.

Hearing his daughters talk about their faith and listening to all the songs that he once loved, I was sure John would fall on his knees and ask for forgiveness. He was surrounded by all that was good when we were together: the friends, the songs, his family, his God. If there wasn't a softening of the heart and a stirring in his spirit that day, I didn't think there ever would be.

There was nothing from him. No apparent remorse, no emotion that I could see. And I think I realized then that he was so set on his path, or maybe even so far down it that he would allow nothing to stop him.

Chapter 21

As a family unit, we were doing okay. Not fantastic, but okay. There were plenty of tears, sadness, and anger. After all, there were three teenage girls and one mother so the hormones alone were enough to cause us rollercoaster days. Add John's leaving to that and there were days that seemed like pure hell.

One thing that was difficult for us all was the sameness of the days. Monday was the same as Saturday, with no real changes or respites for us. Weekends especially were tough because those used to be such family days; Saturdays were always big-breakfast-together days, followed by whatever we wanted to do together. Sometimes it was just working around the house or cleaning up, other times it was walking, hiking or skiing.

Without John it just wasn't the same. But the kids and I did learn from the years with John and from each other, and as the long weekend in May approached, the kids all decided that a camping trip would be fun. Camping in May was something I had always wanted to do, but it had just never seemed to work out. And now, on my own, I didn't think I could do it. I had no idea how to set up our tent, light the lantern, use the camp stove (when we camped, John did all the set up and cooking). Nonetheless, the kids managed to talk me into it.

We packed everything up, including the dog, and off we went camping. Four kids, a mom, and a dog. In a tent. In May. In Canada.

The kids managed to get our large two-room tent set up as well as a smaller tent for our supplies. We were feeling pretty smug that we were tenting together. Until that night when the temperatures dropped to close to the freezing mark!

That first night we ended up wearing our clothes and snuggling with each other and still just about froze to death. To top it all off, we woke up to the sound of rain. We hadn't put up a tarp, because we didn't actually have one, so the rain we heard was right on our tent.

It was a beautiful sound, but that meant it was not warm and sunny out there; we were all pretty sure that it was downright cold, in fact. On a normal camping trip, John would get up before all of us and make a pot of tea. This particular morning, there was no tea and everyone was too cold to get out. Eventually we all out-waited Caitlin and she braved the rain to start a fire. Eventually I had to get up to make the tea, but that wasn't so bad with the fire blazing already.

We ended up going back home for more blankets that day, but then we had the greatest weekend ever. We did all sorts of relaxing things. Connor took me mountain biking, we walked the beach together; we roller-bladed, and the kids even swam!

We had entered a new phase of our healing - creating new memories together. Somewhere I read a quote that sums up this time in our life. "You have to create new memories when someone you love is gone." I'm pretty sure that quote was meant for the widow or widower, but it certainly applied to our situation. John might not have died, but he was most definitely gone from our lives. And so we began slowly to make new memories, new rituals, new traditions, as well as keeping the ones that worked well for us.

The next upcoming milestone was John's and my anniversary. It would have been our 20th and I just couldn't let it pass without some sort of recognition. We'd always been big on anniversaries, birthdays, etc. Before John left, I had already been planning the party I was going to throw to celebrate our 25th anniversary!

I spent a lot of time thinking about how to commemorate this particular day. After all, 20 years was a milestone. Without our marriage, we wouldn't have had these four children and I believed they were more than worth celebrating. I thought about all sorts of different ways of celebrating, from taking the kids away to just going out for dinner. None of the options seemed right, so I threw the question to the kids. They helped me decide to throw a "Happy 20th Un-Anniversary Party."

For women only, of course.

And so the night of what would have been a hugely romantic and special time became one of incredible laughter and friendship. Thirteen ladies came out to help me "celebrate," and in the spirit of the event, brought gifts: everything from flowers and cards to wine and plants. None of us had ever been to an un-anniversary party before and we laughed as they shared thoughts on what one brings to such an event. Hallmark definitely does not cover it. (Turns out there's a huge market they don't even begin to touch!) Even though having an Un-anniversary Party is not something we really would hope would catch on, it was great fun. Once again, I marveled at the blessing of friendships God had given me.

Those events, the camping and the party, were definitely highlights during the first few months, times where we could see God working so incredibly in our lives. Yet the pain was always just below the surface, and would show up at the least expected times, plunging me into the reality of what my life had become and worse, what John's had become.

The secret of his homosexuality was tearing away inside me, causing the most incredible anguish, because I did not know what to do with it. I was beginning to feel like David in the Bible, tossed about, alternately praising God and crying out in fear.

May 27, 2001 journal entry: *Well, I discovered what John's realities are. I thought he was coming around. I truly believed that he was beginning to see the light, to miss us and want to make things good again. When we met the other day, he hugged and kissed me and I really thought he was rethinking his family. Turns out he was simply in the flush of afterglow, having brought his reality closer to home.*

I am sick. I only slept a few hours last night so I knew today could be scary. But I am sick over him. Oh, please, God, can you not take this away? How can this ever end good? Why must I feel such hurt? How do I know the proper way to be? There's no precedent for this in your word. God, am I angry? What is the healthy way for me to get through this? Why, God, why? I'm so alone with my burden. I keep thinking you might want me to share it, but why? So I'll feel better? So someone knows exactly what I'm living through? Can't you just let him die so it's really over? I'm so scared, God, for the kids.

I didn't know how much I still loved him until today. How I was willing to take him back at all costs.

A few days later I wrote another letter to John.

Dear John,

I wanted to write you a letter today just thanking you for all the things you've given me, all the things you were for me. But as I think about each item on my "thankful list" it is balanced by an action on your part that took the joy away from me.

I am thankful for our four children...but you left them with me fatherless, broken-hearted, and wounded.

I am thankful for the love we shared...but you left me thinking I just wasn't enough.

I am thankful for the talks we shared...but I wonder now if you ever really shared.

I am thankful for the friendship we had...but then I realize that real friends don't lie to each for 20 years nor hurt each other like you hurt me.

I am thankful for the happiness you gave me...but it made the sadness so much sadder.

I am thankful that you gave me the opportunity to be a stay-at-home mom and to home-school our children...but now I'm carrying the burden of being a full-time mom and dad, alone in the struggles.

I am thankful you found yourself...but the cost of that discovery was five lives.

I am thankful that you are content...but then I am struck that I was never able to give you that.

I am thankful you are true to yourself...but now that is all you have.

Chapter 22

July of 2001 started a series of events that eventually would unravel the secret. It began to fall apart with a phone call from my dad. He asked how I was and we exchanged all the usual small talk.

Suddenly he seemed to get nervous, as though he was trying to say something but couldn't quite get it out. Finally he told me that people in Chilliwack were wondering if John left me because he was gay. Dad went on to say he knew that was not possible, but he thought he'd just tell me so that I could assure him that it was just one of those nasty rumors that people spread. Hearing my dad say the word "gay" was so much more than I was prepared to deal with that it took me a bit to realize what he was saying. Did my dad just say the word gay? Then it all hit me. There were rumors about John being gay 500 km away from us among a community that we hadn't been part of for 20 years.

I just knew this was not an idle thought that passed by Dad; he was very concerned, but was trying not to let me know or scare me.

I was in my bedroom at the time of our conversation, sitting in a chair in the corner. As it all came together - hearing my dad say gay and realizing the impact of it, I felt as if everything was slowly closing in on me. The room seemed to get smaller and smaller until I could only feel the space directly around me. I could feel myself sliding off the chair and sinking to the carpet. I could hear my heartbeat in my head, like pounding waves on a shore, and I knew I had to end the conversation.

Somehow I found something inside me to assure my dad that, no, of course John was not gay, that he didn't leave me because of that. My dad seemed reassured and we hung up.

I began to cry and shake with the understanding that if people who hardly knew John thought (or knew) he was gay, it would only be a matter of time before people here would hear that rumor or wonder about it themselves.

It seemed so sudden that I had to face the whole issue of John's homosexuality becoming public. I started to wonder about the decision that I had made to protect the kids. Was this actually protecting them? I knew telling them was going to cause all sorts of pain, confusion, and even humiliation, and who wants to cause that for their children? But I had to be completely honest and realize that it would also cause those things for me. I would have to explain over and over that my husband was actually gay. There was a measure of embarrassment that goes with that.

July 15, 2001 journal entry: *I feel like I am going over the edge with all that's happening...I think I may go talk to Dan [elder in our church] soon. I'm quite scared...Through it all, God blesses. I'm just not sure how much more He'll require of me and whether I have it to give. When I think of what may yet come I get so scared.*

The very next day I went to get a hair cut and my hairdresser, a friend from church, told me she saw John recently, walking with a man. I don't know what my face showed her, but she seemed to quickly backpedal and say that maybe it wasn't him, after all; she had only really seen their backs.

I knew it was John and his new partner. At this point, he was in a relationship with a man who lived close by.

It looked like God was showing me that this secret was going to be exposed whether or not I wanted it to be. And that left me, as usual, wondering how I could protect my children. I had no clue what to do.

I knew I had to talk to someone and so I went to see Dan. Dan was the elder that had told John that what was about to enter his home was far worse than an intruder and would destroy his children back when John and I went to tell the elders of our separation. John and I had been attending his bible study and we both considered him to be very wise. God knew exactly who and what I'd need when I finally chose to expose the secret, and so sitting across from Dan I said the words out loud for the first time. "John is gay and that is the real reason he left our marriage." Dan was wonderful in listening to me, not judging the fact that John was gay or that I had tried to keep it a secret. He might not even have been surprised, I don't know. But telling him and knowing that someone would be praying specifically now was such a huge load off me.

July 24, 2001 journal entry: *I've slowly been prepared by God for the next step – complete honesty – where I have, since January, flat out refused to go. Let go, Gerty, and let God. It seems like the things we don't let go of become like a growing octopus. In my bible today I found the verses in Hebrews 12 that say, "Let us throw off everything that hinders and the sin that so easily entangles, and let us run with perseverance the race marked out for us. Let us fix our eyes on Jesus......strengthen your feeble arms and weak knees. Make level paths for your feet...make every effort to live in peace with all men and to be holy...see to it that no one misses the grace of God and that no bitter root grows up to cause trouble and defile many."*

"Let go and let God" began to be something I had to repeat to myself quite regularly. Someone gave me the following beautiful words around that time that really helped me while I was struggling to handle it all.

My Child,

I see how hard you strive to be a good person, but I long for you to know the joy of letting go. Striving as you do is going at it from the wrong direction. It is using external, fleshly efforts to produce internal, spiritual results. I am your internal source of power. When you live and move and have your being in me, life is so much simpler. The changes you yearn for will flow out of your relationship with me. When you let go and give my Spirit permission to take charge, there is freedom and peace and joy on the journey. Cease striving and know me, for I am the One whose hand is on your life. I am the One whose mercy turns your planet. I am the One who yearns to set you free...BE STILL AND KNOW THAT I AM GOD.

There wasn't much doubt left in my mind as the days went by that we had to tell the kids before they found out some other way. I knew that telling them would open a wound that was barely starting to heal over; it would burst wide open again and if we weren't careful, the healing would come to a halt. I dragged my feet in making that decision.

August 16, 2001 journal entry: *The biggest struggle or control issue is when and how we tell the kids the issues that unfortunately they need to know...yesterday I cried from 2:30 p.m. to 12:30 a.m.*

I've come to the conclusion that I am often harsh with John because I don't know who I am around him. I do so well with just the kids or with my friends because I know who I am in that relationship. With John, I don't have a place. Maybe once I can figure that out, I can be kinder. I need to learn to control my anger with him.

Late in August, while wrestling with the decision of how and when to tell our kids, I took them to a nearby city for their annual parade and fall fair. The girls had gone to get our traditional donuts to eat while watching the parade while I kept our places. They came back and said they had run into dad who was out walking with a friend.

They had no clue what they had seen. Or at least that's what I told myself.

I knew the time had come. Too many things were happening and having our children find out their dad was gay through any other means but us was unthinkable. John and I decided that we should tell the kids together. We planned to do so on a Saturday in September, just a few weeks away. To me this was a huge thing. Not just for the kids, but for myself, our church, the community.

At this point, though, it was the kids that were foremost on my mind. As such, I wanted all my duckies in a row again. Just like when we told them we were separating, I knew I needed to be with them after we told them their dad was gay, possibly even more so this time because it was just them and me and it was also the kind of news that none of us had ever heard of another family hearing, so who would know what would happen? That left me in a bit of a quandary. Once the kids knew that their dad was gay, I couldn't leave them, yet telling my parents and my siblings that John was gay was not something I felt I could do on the phone. It was something that I felt I had to do face to face.

In order to do that and be there fully for the kids, I decided to tell my family on the coast the weekend before telling the kids.

I left the kids at home and drove the 500 km to begin another journey; one that involved repeatedly telling people, "The reason my husband left me and the kids is because he is gay."

It was Sunday night, and the time had come to tell my parents. They had invited their best friends over for a visit, and while I loved visiting with them normally (my second parents, in a way), this evening it was tough, knowing what I had to tell my mom and dad when they left. It seemed to take forever for them to go home, and as soon as they had driven off my mom and dad announced that they were going to bed.

I knew I also had an announcement to make that would quite likely change their plans for a bit and not likely give them a good night's sleep. My heart thudded and I wished I were anywhere else. (Have I already mentioned how beautifully traditional my family is? How there were no divorces in the family? No gay husbands either?) Mom and Dad stood up, ready to head upstairs, when I finally screwed up the courage to say that there was something I needed to tell them. They sat back down, almost as if they weren't really surprised. My heart broke for them for all the pain I was inadvertently causing them.

I told them that the son-in-law that they so loved and spent so much time with actually left me and our entire family because he was gay.

There are some things that I am sure a parent never really wants to hear and that must be right up there. They were already struggling with John leaving our marriage, and this most certainly didn't bode well for helping them get over it.

The next night I had dinner out with two of my sisters and my sister-in-law and I told them the same news. Interestingly enough, they weren't surprised at all; they had, in fact, already suspected as much. This shouldn't have come as a shock to me, considering what my dad had told me on the phone, but the extent of how long they had suspected floored me. They had always thought John might be gay, 20 years earlier even. (This would become something I would hear from far too many people in the upcoming days, weeks and months; apparently I was the only one who never ever suspected that my husband was gay.)

I came home from that dinner and was sitting outside with my mom and dad, going over it all again and trying to help them understand it all when I got a phone call from Sarah who was holding down the fort back home. She was crying, and through her tears managed to tell me that she had just received an e-mail from her dad by accident. It mentioned that he wasn't sure if Sarah was ready to hear the truth about his sexuality.

So there I was, 500 km away from my 17-year-old daughter as she discovered that her dad was gay. Perhaps, in hindsight, that was a good thing, because had I been within driving distance of John that night, I think I might have been capable of murder. Once again my heart was destroyed. Worse than that, I was unable to help her. I couldn't hug her, hold her, talk to her, or comfort her. She was completely alone to deal with it.

I offered to come home immediately, but she insisted she'd be okay until the next day when I was coming home anyway.

The next day I went for a run to get rid of some of the anger that I was feeling towards John for such a careless act. When I came back to my mom and dad's, a couple things were completely out of place. First of all, I found my parents still in their pajamas. The only time I ever saw either of my parents in their pajamas was on their way to the bathroom in the middle of the night. Secondly, they were in the den with their eyes glued to the television set. They were watching television before eight in the morning? Something wasn't right.

It was September 11, 2001.

They were watching an airplane crash into a building, replays of the Twin Towers going down.

It seemed like the whole world had gone completely mad.

Chapter 23

The day I could never have imagined in my wildest dreams arrived. I was driving my four children to their dad's apartment in another city so that he could tell them that he was gay. I'm sorry, but does it get weirder than that? Does anyone ever imagine that that is something that might be in their future? I honestly don't remember what I told them we were going to their dad's for, but I'm pretty sure they knew something was up. Realistically, the kids rarely went there and certainly were never driven there by me. Sarah, of course, knew what was coming.

We all sat awkwardly in his living room and talked for a bit. I was leaving it up to John to tell them; I was only there so that I could hear the words he used and then to be there for the kids.

"I love you so much," he began. "And I hate to have to tell you this, but I'm gay and there's nothing I can do about it. I hope you'll love me for what I am."

Caitlin and Connor both started to cry; Deborah turned her back. Sarah, who had the week to process things a bit, said, "This isn't love, dad. Love is putting other people ahead of you. This is just selfish."

And that was about the sum of it. We drove back to Enderby and the kids each went to different places to deal with it, mostly to their friends. Caitlin and Sarah both wanted to meet up with two of their friends, brothers whose mother was my encouraging friend, Sandra. They all went off to walk and talk, and I fell into Sandra's arms.

With my head on her shoulder, I whispered, "He's gay, Sandra. Gay."

Very quietly she answered as she stroked my back, "I know, Gerty, I know."

In the days to follow the kids all had some very strong reactions. Connor refused to talk about it, plugging his ears or covering them if I would even mention his dad. Deb began writing some very dark poetry and Sarah told me that she was feeling quite dead inside. It would be a slow crawl for us all.

And so our lives took a new turn. Bit by bit people found out. It wasn't long before the community was talking about it, which was only to be expected, especially as he was still the manager of the credit union, so quite a prominent part of the community. Who wouldn't talk about that?

Even though it wasn't my actions that would be causing the talk, I was the one that people would wonder about and feel sorry for. Strangely enough, as the weeks went by, I was also the one that everyone seemed to want to talk to about it. I suppose it's quite a normal thing, wanting to know details about the craziest thing they might have heard of in a long time.

If I had a dollar for every time someone asked me if I knew, or how I could not have known in 20 years of marriage that my husband was gay, I'd be one of the wealthier women around. I started to wonder myself. If it was that apparent to everyone else that John might have been gay, how could I not have known?

I mean, sure, he enjoyed shopping with us, he didn't mind cooking, used to do macramé and did, in fact, teach me to knit at one point. But that was just who he was. My dad was a former baker and now a musician; there wasn't a hunter or fisherman in the family, and I had three older sisters. I just wasn't hung up on the stereotypical roles of men and women. I thought he was just a very sweet husband when he did all those things that others might have seen as signs of being gay; to me he was miles ahead of all those stereotypical men, a breath of fresh air.

Besides, how many women really spend time thinking about what kind of strange sexual things her husband might secretly desire? How many wives look at their husbands and wonder if there's something they are hiding from them? It's just not part of a normal marriage (I hope).

Everything was now out in the open. I no longer had to cover for John, hide things, or hope that no one would ever find out the secret. That had to be a positive step, even if it was only the first step on the bottom of the ladder. Yet in the next couple weeks I got kicked off the ladder completely.

I was having what I thought was a routine visit with my doctor when the usual subject came up. John. I felt it was only fair that he knew the truth and so I told him that John was gay. He looked at me a little strangely (that wasn't so unusual, I was getting used to that look). Then he began to question me on our sexual history and finally asked me if I'd been tested for HIV.

Oh, dear Lord, that had never occurred to me. He went on to tell me that the virus can take months to show up, and my mind started reeling with dates and numbers and questions. John had told me, during those five weeks between telling me he was gay and when he actually left, that the man he had left me for was HIV positive. He had also told me that while we were married he had engaged in risky sexual behavior. Truth is I didn't really even know what that meant and never gave it much thought until now.

My doctor thought it would be best if I get tested.

Will it never end, I wondered? Was it not enough that my husband lied to me for 20 years, then decided he would prefer to be gay than to be married to me? Wasn't finding out he was unfaithful to me enough? Wasn't having to tell four children and your parents that your husband was a homosexual not sufficient torture?

I had already dealt with an STD, surely I had done my part of bearing the fallout, hadn't I? Now I had to add to all that the fact that the man I had loved all those years might have infected me with HIV?

I chose not to think about it; I would have the test done and deal with the results. I didn't have anything left to even think about what HIV would mean.

October 18, 2001 journal entry: *Sitting here in the Vernon Jublilee Hospital. I drove Sandra in to have her CT scan and while she was there, I went across the hall and gave blood for my HIV test. I felt like some sex junkie who's now in danger of the consequences. I wanted to scream and tell the technician that I was a faithful Christian but my husband just decided to embrace his homosexuality. Of course I said nothing and just felt like a bad character. A week to ten days and the results will be in....who would have thought this would happen 20 years ago?*

Chapter 24

The tests came back negative, but the feelings I had while sitting in that hospital chair never left me. The sordidness of what I had to experience as a result of the actions of what was supposedly my best friend was just mind boggling at times. It was difficult to make sense of it all, and there were days that I simply had to accept the fact that I might never make sense of it or understand even a part of what was now my life.

While I might not have been able to come to a full understanding, I knew I had to continue to grow, to look to the future, to deal with my pain and my circumstances. To help me, I immersed myself in books. Books that could help me, mostly what I called God Books. There were so many in the first year or two that touched me in a special way. During this difficult time, in particular, while everything was so new and foreign to me, I was reading Jim Smoke's book, *Growing through Divorce*. This book was an eye-opener for me, in that I came to realize that I could choose to let this whole situation make me become a battered, bruised, and bitter statistic...or let this situation be a growth-producing experience in my life. This book gave me practical thoughts and help for taking responsibility, learning to forgive, and letting go.

Someone I Love is Gay was the only book I could find at the time that dealt specifically with homosexuality and how to respond to it, based on others' experiences. This book gave me perspective and an understanding of sorts, but I felt it was not nearly enough for the spouse. The day to day, how to live again advice that I so needed.

31 Days of Praise by Ruth Myers was recommended to me early in my journey and it helped me focus each day on praising God. It helped me gain a spiritual perspective in the middle of hard times.

One of the more powerful books I read was one on forgiveness and it became a book that my girls read as well. *When Forgiveness Doesn't Make Sense*, by Robert Jeffress, gave us all an idea of what to do with exactly that. How do we forgive when it just doesn't make sense to? This is one book that I would recommend to anyone who has been in a circumstance of pain that has nothing to do with them and everything to do with forgiveness. It is freeing.

Even books that didn't have anything to do with God were obviously used by Him. Robert Kiyosaki's book *Rich Dad, Poor Dad* had some really good insights. One thing I learned from that book was that there were so many things I could change about myself even when I couldn't change anything about anyone else. Another gem was to learn to use my emotions to think, not to think with my emotions.

Over and over I had to be so careful what I would let into my mind. I constantly had to battle things that seemed to make sense but didn't line up with the Bible. Like John telling me that God condoned same-sex relationships. I had to repeatedly go back to the basics: Is God who He says He is? Is His word absolute truth? If the answer to both of those is yes, and I believe it is, then I can go to Him and to the Bible for the answers, knowing that everything he says and promises is truth.

All around us we were surrounded by people who loved us, who wanted to help us. Some of those outpourings of help were directly related to John being gay, which I found amusing.

I think what was on most peoples' minds, in those first couple months after the honesty, was Connor. "Poor guy, growing up with three sisters, a mom and being home-schooled; now his dad turned out to be gay." There were a lot of people that were scared that Connor wouldn't become a real man (okay, I might have been one of them at the time) and wanted to do everything they could to help him.

Two of those people were men in my neighborhood, Ken and Sheldon. They had watched for years as their kids played road hockey with Connor and even played some with him themselves at times, and so together they approached me, asking if they could put Connor into real hockey. You know, the Canadian kind – on ice. After much deliberation, several phone calls to friends and family that had already started the hockey journey, I decided it would be fun for him. It would be good for him to have something all his own, something so not-female.

He took to it like, well, a Canadian boy to hockey! It instantly became a family outing each weekend, going to the rink. We all loved watching him play, cheering him on, eating chips (always jalapeno cheddar), and drinking hot chocolate. We felt so Canadian.

I was born to be a hockey mom. A few months after Connor began to play, I decided that I wanted to be a hockey mom in the truest sense of the word. I was already the kind that warmed the bench, lived with the hockey bag stench, got up at outrageous hours and drove wherever was needed. Now, however, I wanted to join the elite of hockey moms – moms who don't just watch; they also play!

Enderby had a women's hockey team; a real coach-included kind of team and I decided to join them. There were 16 players who by day were teachers, doctors, nurses, and moms; and one very brave male coach.

My first experience with hockey began early in the day when I had to be taught how to put my gear on. As much as I wanted to be Superwoman, I had to ask my 11-year-old son for direction. Putting on the socks and the shin pads and chest pad was easy. The pants were a little tougher because I had to keep loosening the laces further and further. And a little further yet. (The comment was heard, but later denied vehemently, "Uh, looking a little hippy there, mom.") Then came the skates. With all the padding, bending over required serious yoga, which I no longer had time to enroll in, and I worked up quite a sweat just getting them on.

By the time I got to the arena, I knew how to get all my gear on and so when I got onto the ice that first night, I thought I looked pretty good. That was before I had to do the hockey thing, though. Our first drill was an easy one – line up on the red line. I found my way there without help, but then the coach told us to skate to the blue line, stop, come back to the red line, stop, etc. Stop? How do you stop? Didn't he know the ice was slippery? I began to sweat. Things were going as well as could be expected when the coach instructed us to go backwards and cross our skates over each other. At the same time! I couldn't help myself and I blurted out, "You're joking, aren't you?"

He wasn't.

As the evening progressed, I did not. I did discover that only in women's hockey, when you can't stop on your own, you can do it by employing a full-contact hug. Or, when you don't have time to extend your arms, simply with full contact.

Hockey became something that Connor and I shared. I'd come home from practice late at night and go check up on him in bed. He would often semi-wake up and ask me if I had scored any goals. It was a long time before I could finally tell him that yes, I had scored a goal. (Years later, he would join me for a practice and even help coach the occasional time.)

New traditions and memories were being made and we managed to still feel like a family. Not the same family, but a family nonetheless. A month after we told the kids their dad was gay, on October 17, to be exact, I decided to make a treat for us all, a lemon meringue pie. I suppose I hadn't been doing too much baking of late, but I hadn't realized that until each of my kids walked past that pie and questioned me.

"Are we having company?"

"Is there a reason you made a lemon meringue pie?"

"I guess that's not for us, huh?"

"What's with the pie?"

I figured if they didn't think that I would make a pie just for them, then they deserved to be bugged a little.

And so I answered, "Of course there's a reason for this pie. How could you not know?"

They waited for me to go on. I let them wait a while before I stopped what I was doing and turned to them. "What? Don't tell me you honestly don't know why I made this."

They still looked blank. Which, of course, was logical, because I was truly thinking on my feet, having made it simply as a treat.

"Good grief, guys, have you not looked at the calendar?"

There were a few glances at the calendar and then more confused faces.

"It's October 17, you know...okay, have you never heard of the 17th tradition?...each month on the 17th it's a National Food Day. Yeah, every month. October is National Lemon Meringue Pie Day. Everywhere all over the world, people are making and eating lemon meringue pie. Seriously." They didn't take me seriously and as we got more and more into the idea, another family tradition began. Together we created a year's worth of

National 17th Days and celebrated them faithfully for the next two years.

We had National Morning Day where we'd stay in our pajamas all day and eat only cereal (that one was the most difficult; we all started craving meat by the end of the day!). Then there was National Left Over Valentine's Candy Day, National Lucky Charms for Breakfast Day, National Ice Cream Sundae Day, National Gourmet Ice Cream Day, National Bites of the Round Table Day (which meant we had to have lunch at the food court in the mall and sit at the only round table they had, no matter how long we had to wait), National Cream Puff Day, National Apple Crisp Day, National Pick-a-Purdy's-Chocolate Day, National Homemade Pizza Day and National Go Out for Chinese Food Day.

The kids and I hung on to all the traditions that were there that still worked, but we were a different family now and we needed to mark that difference with new things.

Yet for every small step that we seemed to take forward, there seemed to be half a step taken backwards. The kids had only known about their dad's homosexuality for a month and I knew they were struggling. Sarah was depressed, unable to sleep or concentrate, losing short term memory, struggling with such deep hurts. I am sure some of that came from John telling her that he wished he'd not taught her Christianity but more humanism. For a girl who chose to follow Christ because of what her dad and mom taught her, this was an enormous load to carry.

Deborah was still writing dark poetry and not doing much in the way of school work. Connor cried at night, not understanding times when his dad canceled their plans or didn't return his calls. It was difficult for me to help the kids, as there was so much I didn't understand myself. I just knew that if I loved them and was there for them, they might have a fighting chance in coming through this all in a positive way. While I was dealing daily with the fallout of John's coming out he informed me that he would be moving in with his partner and wanted Connor to meet him.

That sent me reeling. (Is there a word for reeling again when you're already reeling?) Connor was just 11 years old, completely sheltered and innocent. I'm not even sure he knew the reality of what homosexuality was. All my motherly alarm bells went off. Where did this partner come from, how did I know my son was safe with him, how would Connor react to seeing his dad hug and kiss a man or watch him go to bed with a man at night?

I knew there was no curriculum in our home-school that covered that.

I also knew with every fiber of my being that I needed to protect him from that at that point. There was nothing positive to be gained for Connor, at 11 years old, by meeting his dad's partner. It was not a vindictive thought against John; it was purely for Connor's well-being.

A few weeks later, I felt that I needed help to fight this and went to see a lawyer to find out if and how I could protect him; if I had any rights whatsoever to deny John access to him.

Because all of this was so foreign to me, I did some research on the whole issue of homosexuality and molestation. What I read did not make me feel at all better about bringing in a stranger to Connor's life. From what I read, there seemed to be a higher percentage of molestation between homosexual men and boys. Some studies showed that often a boy who is molested chooses a homosexual lifestyle later on in life Again, because everything was uncharted territory for me, I didn't feel it at all inappropriate to ask for John's partner to undergo a criminal check. I needed to know my son would be safe.

For whatever reason, John delayed moving in with his partner. It would happen in the new year, he informed me. I insisted on Connor not meeting his new partner at this point, and John honoured that.

Another battle was only just beginning.

Chapter 25

Before we knew it we were facing our first Christmas without John. In many ways, of course, we were dreading it. We all knew that it wouldn't be the same as before and I think we were all quite nervous about how it would all turn out.

I made a point to keep things as lively and normal as I could for the kids, but many of the pre-Christmas rituals were lonely times for me. Christmas was always a time that John and I loved. We had hosted parties together every year, whether it was the credit union Christmas party or one after the Sunday School concert. We did so many of the traditions together: buying gifts, getting the tree, filling stockings, staying up late to make sure everything was ready. Things the kids may never have even been aware of that go into making Christmas. It was definitely not a do-it-alone kind of holiday for me.

That year we went with our neighbors, Ken and Lori to get a tree and on the way we listened to the usual Kenny Rogers and Dolly Parton Christmas music (it's tradition). As much as I wanted to be that Superwoman again, I had to ask Ken to help us set the tree up. But the decorating we did all by ourselves. Keeping with tradition, we toasted our tree with eggnog when it was all decorated and had our usual family party. When the kids had all gone to bed, I sat with just the lights of the tree on and remembered the desperation of the year before when I'd given John my wedding ring and how badly I'd hoped that the next year would be different.

I guess I received what I hoped for. It was definitely different.

Just not the kind of different I had in mind.

December 19, 2001 journal entry: *Another letter to you, John. This morning, Deborah told me that you and your partner would be serving Christmas dinner at the April House [a shelter for women]. I find it ironic that you are volunteering to help women who probably come there because a man has hurt them, either physically or emotionally. Just like you did. As you look into the haunted faces of these women and children and kindly give them food, I hope the faces of your wife and children look back at you...tell them your story, John, watch their reactions. Tell them about your beautiful wife, your four wonderful children, your great friends, and lovely home. Then tell them how you left it all to live the gay life. Ask them if they still want you to serve them. Look in the eyes of the children. See the pain, the hurt, the lack of trust. It's the same as your children's eyes. Know that you put the pain there, caused the hurt, the lack of trust. God forgive you, John, for what you've done.*

Christmas Day journal entry, 11:40 p.m.: *Our first Christmas as a new family, as a single mom. I told the kids last night to get up any time after seven this morning and at 6:59 Connor poked me on the shoulder. At 7:01 all the kids were in my bed wishing each other a merry Christmas. At 7:15 we all got up and got ready to open gifts – teeth and hair brushed. Connor wouldn't brush his teeth because it wasn't "natural enough then." At 7:30 we posed in front of the tree for a self-timed photo and then we all joined hands and prayed for God's blessing on our day for Him. Then, one by one, we opened our gifts. We all enjoyed seeing each others' gifts, giving ours and receiving. After all the gifts were open we sat down to our breakfast on china plates. We lounged around a bit, I got the turkey stuffed and in the oven (first time all by myself) and prepared some dinner stuff. In the afternoon we met a group of friends at Gardom Lake to skate. The sky was blue, the lake was glass. You could see the seaweed and even a fish through it – it was amazing!*

We had company for dinner, played a game, and then after they left, the kids and I watched a Christmas video. It was an incredible day, an unbelievable day. God blessed us beyond our wildest dreams.

The new year began with a heavy heart for me, trying to decide what was best for Connor and how to allow him to be a child for as long as possible. I decided that the first thing I should do was at least meet John's partner. I trusted my instincts about people, so my thinking was that at least I'd have an idea of what kind of man he was. We agreed to have lunch with the three of us. As I walked into the restaurant, I saw John and his partner both sipping their drinks through little green straws. I found this almost comical and yet sad, how flamboyant they both looked.

The conversation began quite nicely; a lot of small talk about cars, kids. It was a pleasant conversation and I was not feeling anything at all that would alert me to danger. This man seemed genuinely friendly and easy to talk with, a likeable guy.

After a while he asked me about why I wanted a criminal check done. Was it because he was gay, he wondered? I answered him truthfully that, yes, in fact, it was; I didn't know him or where he's been, and I needed to protect my son (I didn't tell him that, based on John's decision to have "risky sex" with an HIV positive partner, I didn't trust John's judgment.) To the best of my ability I was rational, kind, calm, and even understanding. I pointed out to him that I was concerned about some of the research I did and how the Boy Scouts organization at that time wouldn't accept gay men as leaders because of issues of molestation, so there was a bit of a reality that I felt I had to address.

He simply answered, "They're just bigots."

Trying a different tactic, I explained the responsibility I felt in raising a son alone – the responsibility given to me by John leaving. I explained how, as a Christian, I couldn't give up my beliefs and morals just because John appeared to have.

John and his partner, in turn, explained that if Connor were to be around them, they would simply expand his worldview to help him make choices. And if one of those choices would be to be gay, they asked, wouldn't it be better for him to live a life of honesty instead of how John lived?

I'll admit to a few alarm bells going off then.

Just before the partner left angry and without a goodbye because he "refused to get into an argument or continue this further," he let me know that he thought I was a bigot, full of hate and if he had children, he would never let them in my Christian home.

I asked him what I had said that made him think I hated him, but he didn't give me an answer.

February 2, 2002 journal entry: *I am so scared because I know I don't stand a chance in court and that is where we'll have to go next. If I give in, Connor loses. If I fight, Connor loses. What do I do to help Connor get the best? I think I need to back off and let Connor meet his dad's partner. And just pray. Just the thought of that makes me cry. How can John justify these actions? How can he be so willing to sacrifice his son for his sexuality? Will God intervene?*

In an effort to make the right decision I contacted several people who might have some insight in the matter, organizations that would understand what I was dealing with. It was pretty straight across with the advice. I was told I should fight.

Still hoping I didn't need to go that route, I asked John to meet for me for coffee and there I tried again to explain calmly where I was coming from. The points I made were:

- I did not want to keep him from having a relationship with any of his children.
- If the girls wanted to meet his new partner, I would not interfere at all.
- My biggest concern was that Connor was too young to deal with the realities of homosexuality and needed to be protected from it until he was of an age and maturity to understand it and cope with the impact of it.

John was angry and wouldn't hear me. He was going away for several weeks and so I determined within myself to make a decision before he returned.

February 18, 2002 journal entry: *One whole year since John left. Yesterday marked the date exactly and so I went before the church and thanked them for their prayers and let them know how blessed I felt to be part of this church and how I loved them all. A year. One year later I am a stronger, more confident woman.*

I decided to take one step at a time and wait. If God allowed that one and made it clear that it was okay, I would take another step.

A few weeks later, John came back. We had coffee together and he informed that he was moving in with his partner.

He also told me he was proceeding to divorce me.

Chapter 26

Wow. Those were not words that I ever expected to hear my husband say. Even though we were separated, hearing him say that he was going to divorce me hurt me deeply, and took me completely by surprise. Realistically, there was no reason for it. It wasn't likely that he'd be getting married again. The only conclusions I could make was that he either wanted his freedom from me utterly and completely or he simply wanted to hurt me. Neither option felt good.

And so John moved in with his partner. I did not want Connor to go to his house; not until, at the very least, a criminal check had been done on his partner (which he steadfastly refused to do). However, I did not stop John and Connor from getting together. I knew this made it very awkward for John, always having to take Connor out to do something, rather than hang out in his home, and I was sorry that it had to be that way, but at this point, that was what I felt was necessary and healthiest for Connor. I repeatedly explained to John, even in writing, how his homosexuality was a difficult thing for the kids to deal with. I told him how I encouraged the girls to come to terms with our marriage breaking up and with his homosexuality. My desire for them was to go through healthy emotional and spiritual healing so that they'd be able to maintain healthy relationships as adults.

I had the same desires for Connor. I felt that we owed him a childhood free from controversial adult issues that he was not ready to deal with. As his mother, I truly felt that I had to encourage his relationship with John, whatever that took. However I believe he needed to grow up and mature before he had to deal with the issue of his dad's homosexuality. I believed that the issue was way too big for an eleven-year-old.

I believed that it was my responsibility to help Connor heal from his pain, to do everything possible for him to have a healthy and good relationship with John. I also believed that could all happen without any exposure to his dad's homosexuality and lifestyle at that point.

If we did our job well, he would be able to face it all in a healthy way, accepting it as a part of his dad. But in order for that to happen, I felt that he needed to be tended to gently with huge amounts of love and reassurance. There would be a lifetieme of a good strong relationship between them if we could allow him his childhood.

I so wanted John to understand this. Not necessarily agree, but understand.

June 5, 2002 journal entry: *On May 22, what would have been our 21ˢᵗ wedding anniversary, I was served divorce and access papers. On June 7 I have to go to court. It's been two weeks since I got the papers. There was such a quiet peace the first week, then one day I was suddenly struck with the thought that my best friend was choosing to divorce me. That was a tough day.*

This past weekend I met Joanne, Tiffany, Coreen and Lori [some of the same friends who threw me my 40ᵗʰ birthday party] in Kelowna to see Liz Curtis Higgs and Carol Kent. It was an incredible conference and there was a healing there for me. A real sense of having only God, but He was enough.

A comment was made during the conference that children see their heavenly father as they see their earthly father. I knew I couldn't give a positive picture of that to my kids and I began to cry. Joanne put her arm around me and after a while, I felt another hand on my shoulder. I thought it was Tif or Lori but then I heard Tif singing and it was no where near me. So I glanced over my shoulder and there was no one there! I believe

God's hand was there and He was comforting me in such an incredible feeling of loss.

This week leading up to the court case has been one of feeling cleansed and whole and healed. I feel like a burden has been lifted. I can't explain how it feels. My husband is divorcing me, fighting me for access of our son, I am going broke to fight it, and he's still gay. Yet I have never been more content.

I don't know what this Friday will bring in court. I do know that groups of Christians all over B.C. will be praying for me. I stand amazed and awed. May I never lose this feeling.

The only time I had ever been in a court room was to watch a ceremony welcoming our Japanese exchange students to the country several years earlier. Now I was going to court to be tried (at least that's what it felt like). After all my legal duckies were in a row and everything was organized, I was left with the dilemma of what to wear. You might be laughing, but it was a serious issue for me. Not only was I going to court, but I was going in there to show that I was a responsible and caring mother, not a lunatic or homophobic woman (which I had every chance of being perceived as). Not only that, I would be coming out of there a divorcee. Is there an outfit appropriate to cover that, I ask you?

Eventually I went shopping and bought a proper blouse to wear with my responsible motherly black pants.

That Friday I walked up the steps of the old courthouse and then into the Supreme Court of British Columbia. The courthouse was built at the turn of the twentieth century, majestic and architecturally beautiful. And completely intimidating to me. Just walking into a building so rich in history made me feel like everything done within these walls was serious business. I was a little scared.

The Supreme Court was every bit as grand as you'd expect from that era. Resplendent with rich, dark wood, I was awed. My lawyer and I sat at one of the ancient heavy wooden tables, on the main level. The judge's seat was on a separate level above us, behind a gleaming wooden railing. As we waited for the judge to enter we spoke in hushed voices. We were all asked to rise as the judge came into the room, walked up several steps and sat behind his desk, looking down at us. Dressed in robes and looking quite somber, it was a serious and formal affair.

The judge listened to John's request for access to Connor, then listened to my reasons for withholding some of that access. His ruling was that we all had to do what was best for Connor and what was best for Connor was to not have him around John's partner. At all, he said. He then ordered that ten days from then I was to take Connor to his dad's and the three of us were to have dinner together. This was in order to set my mind at ease with the surroundings and to reassure myself that John's home would be a safe and healthy place for Connor.

If all was in order, the judge believed Connor could safely spend time at his dad's home, but did go on to order that John's partner was not to be present at any access visits until a further court order, and there were to be no overnight visits with Connor and his dad. Those would commence on dates that John and I would agree on the following month.

June 8, 2002 journal entry (the day after court): *Everyone was praying. There was so much I wanted to say but I was held back by those prayers and that was good. The hardest thing was watching John put his hand on the Bible and declare our marriage over with no hope for reconciliation. I cried. When the judge asked me if that's how I felt, I said that no, this was not my desire but neither was it in my control. I wouldn't oppose it. The marriage was over and to watch him say that with his hand on the Bible hurt more than I ever thought possible.*

Three days later an amazing thing happened. John gave me a card telling me how sorry he was. He didn't say for what and it wasn't important that it be specific. It meant a lot to me that he was sorry.

June 10, 2002 journal entry: *I had to forgive. Not for him, but for me. I sent him a card with a printed thank you, and on the inside I wrote "I forgive you." I am counting on God to do the rest. I will remember that I don't need to forget the offense, but I do need to remember my decision to forgive. It's a choice I made.*

I choose today to get better, not bitter.

Our court-ordered dinner (does it get any weirder than that?) was nice. I felt that the environment was okay; I didn't see or feel anything out of the ordinary that would give me concerns for Connor and so he began going to John's house twice a week for visits.

Three months later we were headed back to court. I was trying to keep Connor from having to meet John's partner. The morning of that court appearance I was reading in Psalms and a passage jumped out at me:

"If an enemy were insulting me,
I could endure it;
If a foe were raising himself against me,
I could hide from him.
But it is you, a man like myself,
my companion, my close friend,
with whom I once enjoyed sweet fellowship
as we walked with the throng at the house of God."
Psalm 55:12-14

And so I faced another court appearance against the person who used to be my companion, my close friend. It was pretty much the same format as the one before, with the judge listening to both sides. He then declared that there didn't seem to be any more compromise and said that we should take it to a hearing. That was to happen October 1.

My lawyer recommended that Connor see a psychologist to determine his readiness to meet the partner. With some fear I agreed. I was scared because it appeared that a psychologist would be the one to determine Connor's maturity, based on a two-hour visit. Not so much based on how he was raised, his spiritual upbringing or the morality our family lives by. Regardless of all of that, however, I trusted that this was the best option.

The choice of psychologist was limited to those that were approved by the court to make decisions for the court and as such we didn't really have a choice. There was only one that was available and so we booked an appointment.

Connor and I met with the psychologist. Connor hated it and wanted nothing to do with him, but he knew he didn't have a choice so he sat there and answered his questions. I got the impression that we were simply an easy paycheque for this doctor. He was sanctimonious, condescending, and didn't seem to have a grasp on the realities of a family unit as I knew it, and the effect of disruption to it on a young child.

We received the psychologist's report concerning Connor's wishes in relation to ongoing access with his dad, and his opinion as to how that should be structured.

The doctor's recommendations were that Connor be allowed to have dinner with his dad and his partner after more counseling, but no overnights for a year or two. He also stated that overt displays of affection should be held in abeyance for the foreseeable future, and that Connor did not require detailed information concerning his father's homosexuality.

This report didn't sit too well with John and through his lawyer he contacted the psychologist again. As a result of this pressure, another report was given, suggesting that perhaps after three months of weekly dinners with the partner, Connor could stay overnight, but with his dad's partner in a separate bedroom. "Connor is presently not prepared to stay at his father's overnight while his father and partner sleep in the same bedroom."

On October 16, 2002 I wrote another letter to John.

Dear John,

I cannot believe that we have come to the place where we are fighting about whether or not homosexuality is something that should be part of our son's life. For a year now I have struggled with what the consequences would be either way. I haven't just battled you; I have battled society, myself, and God.

I wanted so badly to be your friend, to have you still like me, to approve of me. I so badly wanted to still have you as my best friend. But I could only have those things at the price you determined, and I was not willing to pay. I am sorry for that.

There are no winners in this battle, and the one who stands to lose the most is Connor. All he wants is to be with his dad. His biggest desire is for our family to be whole again, but he knows that you cannot give that to him. The next best thing for him is to have as much time with you as possible.

I have no clue as to how the courts will rule next week. I have no confidence in this world any more – we have an amoral society at best.

I do have confidence that, regardless of the results of our court battle, God will uphold all His promises to me and that He loves and cares for Connor more than you or I ever could. It is in that love and those promises that I rest.

Should I "lose," I will continue to trust that God is in control. He knows what He is doing and I will do everything in my power as a mom to help Connor adjust to the new situation.

I give you my word that I will do whatever is needed for Connor to continue to grow up and mature in a healthy way.

I cannot and will not ever condone your gay relationships – it is contrary to the very core of a functional society, that being the family. However, I will raise Connor to love you always. It's up to you to earn the respect and honour.

I may lose this battle, John, but in God I already know the outcome of the war.

After several postponements the new court date was set for December 10, 2002. In the last week of November my lawyer suddenly found himself in a conflict of interest with my case and had to remove himself from it.

On a Friday afternoon, I called a contact in Vancouver, an activist who had encouraged me to fight against having Connor meet his dad's gay partner. She happened to be in her office and knew of a lawyer that she thought would be perfect. Putting me on hold, she called this lawyer, Patricia, who happened to have the exact dates free when we were scheduled for court; she was willing to come up and be my lawyer. It all fell into place like things can only do if God is in control.

December 10, 2002 journal entry: *Court. My lawyer, Patricia, and John's lawyer went before the judge to file their case. The judge was nervous about the case, said he wasn't sure he could even hear it. He asked where the application was and Patricia told him she didn't see one, but had only been retained since the previous Friday. The judge then asked John's lawyer for it, and he wasn't able to locate it. The judge told him that that wasn't good enough for his courtroom, and that he'd better take this serious and get it together.*

After the hearing, Patricia approached the other lawyer privately and said that she didn't really see a problem here, that dad already had access to the son, and that mom was more than willing to accommodate him. It looked to her like this was about the partner's access so maybe he should make his own application for access.

The result of that day in court was that the court ordered that we attend "conjoint counseling," meaning that John and Connor would go to counseling as well as Connor and I. This was to occur anywhere between one and five times.

Following that, we would see what recommendations were made. And so, in the new year, 2003, that is what we did. John and I met with the counselor together and then each of us went with Connor. The psychologist's report suggested that "Connor is psychologically prepared to engage in a series of activities (e.g. mini golf or inner tubing) with his father and his partner...I see no barrier to this occurring at an early date."

On March 23, 2003, we went back to court and the judge changed the order of the previous June, allowing John's partner to participate in access visits, but not be present for overnight access visits until further court order, meaning he was now allowed to be around Connor, but had to sleep somewhere else.

It was a small victory, but it was one that made me feel Connor was still somewhat protected.

Chapter 27

Life continued to go on in spite of the court battle.

April 9, 2003 journal entry: *So. Sold the house, bought a house, got a job, Sarah's engaged. I think that's about it. Oh, wait. John lost his job and went bankrupt."*

Each one of those happenings could fill a book. Selling and buying a house by myself (with a little help from my dad, my brother and my brothers-in-law) was a whole new world; getting a job for the first time in almost 20 years was intimidating; my oldest daughter meeting a man, falling in love and getting engaged was a new step for us all.

6:15 a.m. Saturday April 26, 2003 journal entry: *I'm sitting in half light wanting to write one last entry of reflection in this house. In a couple hours friends and movers will be here to move us out of here and into our new place.*

Just over five and a half years ago we moved into this house, this town. I suppose it was with great expectations but not searching for a miracle. I know I wanted to have a new start for myself personally and try to be a better person, mom, wife, and friend. I wonder if John hoped at all for some deliverance from his homosexuality. Who knows, because he has also expressed that he knew it was inevitable that he was going to leave me for the gay life. Ironically, I wanted to be better, he was beginning to accept what he thought and thinks was his fate.

Five and a half years later, am I a better person? Has John met his fate? Yes, undoubtedly I am better. I like who I am, what

I do, my relationships, my decisions. As to John's fate – he thinks he's met it.

Five and a half years later I am moving myself and my kids to a new house and a new start again. Mostly for financial reasons, but also for new memories. I love the new house but find myself nervous, scared, and a bit worried. Yet I know this is a total God thing and we are doing exactly what He wants. I will continue to trust Him.

As I sit in this messed up living room one last time, I hope I will be able to release the past in the new house. Move on to a new future. I pray that I can live in joy and forgiveness; that I will continue to grow.

I pray that the kids will adjust and also learn to move forward and grow in themselves.

And now I will rest my pen until we're in the new house.

"Praise God from whom all blessings flow."

Postscript

In July of 2003, the access visits between John's partner and Connor were reviewed yet again, with John having grown impatient with the process. The psychologist then reported that "at present Connor is psychologically equipped to accept Mr. ---- being in the home when he is there overnight so long as his father and Mr ----- do not share the same bed. He is not prepared to spend overnights in the home with his father and his father's partner in the same bedroom...I envision no reason to go beyond the present recommendation for a period of a minimum of 12 months."

On October 21, 2003, the court order was changed to allow John's partner to participate in full access visits, including overnight, but the proposal that the psychologist gave us in July was to be upheld. Until June of 2004 John and his partner would not be allowed to share a bed while Connor was in the home.

Ultimately, of course, that did happen when anticipated and the battle for my son which began in the fall of 2002 ended in June of 2004.

Ultimately the courts of British Columbia, Canada, agreed that an 11-year-old boy was not ready to meet his father's homosexual partner, or to be a witness to his homosexual lifestyle. By the time the psychologist and judges agreed on full access, Connor was almost 14 years old.

As I said in my letter to John on October 16, 2002, "I will continue to trust that God is in control."

I believe He was, He is, and ever will be.

Gerty Shipmaker is available for speaking engagements and personal appearances. For more information contact:

Gerty Shipmaker
C/O Advantage Books
P.O. Box 160847
Altamonte Springs, Florida 32716

To purchase additional copies of this book or other books published by Advantage Books call our toll free order number at:
1-888-383-3110 (Book Orders Only)

or visit our bookstore website at:
www.advbookstore.com

Longwood, Florida, USA
"we bring dreams to life" TM
www.advbooks.com

LaVergne, TN USA
14 October 2010
200850LV00001B/16/P